Business Partnering

A business partner is a professional who supports and advises strategic and operational decision-making through insights that drive better business performance. Often as a result of external changes, business partners must respond quickly to map out the future strategic development, keep the firm competitive and ensure all objectives and legal requirements are met.

In this book, business partnering expert Steven Swientozielskyj introduces a framework that provides a set of practical tools and techniques via a simple six-stage model that, when replicated, will take the practitioner from start to finish through strategic change; from the formation and agreement of the strategy to its delivery and sustainability.

Business Partnering is a one-stop shop for understanding this important phenomenon and as such will be vital reading for practitioners and academics in the business arena.

Steven Swientozielskyj BA (Hons), FCMA, MBA, CGMA, is an international speaker and expert on world-class improvements relating to complex service and change issues.

Business Partnering captures the very best of Steve's own transformational and world-class experience and blends it with the latest research and success stories. Steve has made it available in a readily digestible way for all existing and aspiring practitioners. This wonderful resource is a 'must-have' for all business partners and indeed for anyone where multi-disciplinary teamwork is essential for success.

David Murphy, *Retired Head of HR Services, Network Rail, UK*

Business Partnering is a must-read for professionals seeking to differentiate their practised approach to increase the value of their outputs. This practical handbook has an abundance of concise evidential reference points from numerous theoretical models and frameworks that can be directly applied in professional practices. The author has a leading-edge view on business partnering and this handbook will be my go-to guide for many years to come.

Milgintas Milo Mazeika, *Assistant Management Accountant, Mentee, UK*

Steve has uniquely brought together the various facets of business partnering and structured the content around a six-stage general model. The combination of relevant research and techniques, together with Steve's own real-life case studies, provide an excellent guide for practitioners wishing to enhance their knowledge within organisations. This excellent book provides business partners with the insight necessary to make positive changes within their sphere of influence.

Stephen J. Smith, *Head of Finance Shared Services, Network Rail, UK*

The handbook of business partnering is an authoritative guide for any professional who interacts with stakeholders. The general model provides a framework that all professionals can apply to a multitude of circumstances. I particularly enjoyed the sections on how to develop trust and how to deal with conflict. This sets a new standard and therefore a must-read for those who interact with stakeholders.

David Stanford, *Vice President,*
The Chartered Institute of Management Accountants, UK

Business Partnering is an excellent book which captures how to create a culture of excellence in today's highly competitive environment. By combining key areas into a six-stage model, Steve has provided a real-life useable guide on how to improve organisational performance, teamwork and engagement. Applying Steve's frameworks in my current workplace has already led to a number of success stories. This book will most definitely be by my side throughout my career.

Samantha Risby, *District Manager, Signet, UK*

Business Partnering

A practical handbook

Steven Swientozielskyj

LONDON AND NEW YORK

First published 2016
by Routledge
2 Park Square, Milton Park, Abingdon, Oxon OX14 4RN

and by Routledge
711 Third Avenue, New York, NY 10017

Routledge is an imprint of the Taylor & Francis Group, an informa business

British Library Cataloguing in Publication Data
A catalogue record for this book is available from the British Library

Library of Congress Cataloging-in-Publication Data
Swientozielskyj, Steven.
Business partnering : a practical handbook / Steven Swientozielskyj.
– 1 Edition.
     pages cm
   Includes bibliographical references and index.
   1. Partnership. 2. Industrial management – Technological innovations.
   3. Communication in management. 4. Organizational change. I. Title.
   HD69.S8S95 2016
   658´.042–dc23   2015028342

ISBN: 978-1-138-90799-7 (hbk)
ISBN: 978-1-138-90800-0 (pbk)
ISBN: 978-1-315-69482-5 (ebk)

Typeset in Bembo
by HWA Text and Data Management, London
Printed in Great Britain by Ashford Colour Press Ltd

To my mother Nadia
and my daughters, Debra and Jodie Swientozielskyj

Contents

Figures

Tables

Foreword

This book aims to support organisations that are aware of the need to develop a culture of efficiency, effectiveness and excellence in the highly competitive world of modern global, national and local business; it is equally relevant to large corporates and high growth SMEs, as it identifies the importance of best practice business partnering. This key activity, if undertaken well, will improve the organisation's performance and engagement with a wide range of stakeholders.

The business of successful business partnering is well documented by professional bodies (CIMA, ACCA and CIPD, to name but a few), the big four finance and accounting and consultancy organisations (PriceWaterhouseCooper, Deloitte, KPMG and Ernst and Young) and appears in many corporate publications, as an engagement optimisation solution in the fast moving global environment. Gary Rourke, VP Finance at Astra Zeneca states:

> there is a vital role for business partners to ensure we're making the right calls for strategy and the overall direction of the business.
>
> (Robert Half Netherlands, 2012: 7)

Deloitte state from their research that:

> 83% of Organisations want to increase the time spent on finance business partnering over the next three years.
>
> (Deloitte, 2012: 3)

However, the business partnering role stretches way beyond the finance function.

The approach that this book adopts seeks to identify and outline a six-stage based general model of partnering, applicable to all managers engaged in partnering activities. The text is based on research material, academic and applied business models, case studies and existentialist business peer reviews from leading practitioners, who have implemented programs or have managed business partners within significant, national and international organizations. The outcome can be applied in both the public and private sectors. Business partners and educationalists in the field have also been involved by providing an overview of the text, to ensure the creation of add value and 'real-life' application at the point where strategic and operating models combine with reality to maximise business performance.

Although organizations are implementing more sophisticated and wider business partnering programs, there is at times evidence of a disjointed approach being applied. This misalignment fosters a mediocre orientation and inadequate support process for developing partnering activity and results in poor outputs and outcomes for stakeholders. There is significant though somewhat fragmented material available, within the business partnering literature, but to date no specific or all engaging business partnering 'end-to-end business model' has been developed.

The author provides an 'end-to-end model' for business partnering from the perspective of a comprehensively structured six-stage model for business partnering activity.

It includes the following stages:

- Preparation
- Engagement
- Acceptance
- Delivery
- Change
- Outcome.

Models, methods, tools and techniques that can be applied to optimise business partnering engagement are included in each of the six stages and the relationships between the stages is evidenced. The application of the modular approach will increase the effectiveness of the business partner's positive and transparent engagement with their stakeholders. The text aims to support and create a dialogue for managers and their teams towards the development of business partnering best practice in the global arena.

References

Deloitte LLP (2012) *Changing the Focus: Finance Business Partnering,* Deloitte Publications. http://www2.deloitte.com/content/dam/Deloitte/uk/Documents/finance-transformation/deloitte-uk-finance-business-partnering.pdf.

Robert Half Netherlands (2013) *Business Partnering: Optimising Corporate Performance,* Robert Half Management Report. http://www.roberthalf.nl/EMEA/Netherlands/Assets/cfo-report-2013/Robert-Half-CFO-Report-2013.pdf.

Preface

As the author of this book I am reaching out to the reader and tell you the story of why I wrote this book. The journey of writing this book started when I developed a qualification for my professional institute. I had material which was too complex and did not fit into this project. The question to myself is 'where do I place this great material?'. The answer to the reader was it was the starting point of what is contained with the general model of business partnering and the six stages that I have developed. I hope that the reader will increase their knowledge to enhance their applied skills and competences.

In this journey I have actively looked for peer review from senior stakeholders who demand results, those who have set up business partnering programs, educationalists and indeed business partners, and some of these are named and included in the acknowledgements. In this journey I have changed and learned; with hindsight, what I could have done better in my career, albeit I have had a very successful one. I wish I could have had the knowledge contained in this book much earlier in my career, so why not share this insight. The problem I had writing this book was that in my opinion I faced fragmented parts of a jigsaw. There was no holistic overview of business partnering. My main trial and tribulation was at the mid point of writing this book where I completely changed and redrafted what I had already written; it was too complex and I had too much material, so the challenge was to simplify and condense what was initially drafted.

My experiences have spanned decades of working at senior levels with leading national and international organizations, and the relevant learnings and insights have been part of the research and content that has been included. What has been important to me have been the peer reviews and insights provided by professionals who also have spanned decades of senior roles. They have also developed successful careers. So in summary there are over a hundred man-years of experiences for the reader to learn from. This combined with case studies and research material should make a powerful combination to increase the reader's knowledge. I thank those executives who have 'done it' and have been willing to share their knowledge, skills and competences with you and this is why I have written the book.

Acknowledgements

A special thank you for those who supported the development of this book: David Murphy. MA (Oxon); David Stanford FCMA; Eileen Mary Roddy, BA (Hons) Economics and Social Studies, PGCE, MBA, MSc Educational Management, ICAEW (Intermediate)Member BAFA; George Connell ACMA, CGMA, MBA;Jonathan Potts BEng, FCMA, CGMA; John D Greenwood FCMA,CGMA; Milgintas Milo Mazeika BSc, MSc; Sam Risby BSc.(Hons); Steven John Smith BA (Hons), FCMA,MBA,CGMA; and Susan Jane Swientozielskyj RGN, MSc.

Abbreviations

4C	cash, cycle time, compliance, customer care
5C	company, competitors, customers, collaborators, climate
ADKAR	awareness, desire, knowledge, ability, reinforcement
BI	business intelligence
BPR	business process re-engineering
CIO	chief information officer
EFQM	European Foundation for Quality Management
KPIs	key performance indicators
HR	human resources
IT	information technology
NASA	National Aeronautics and Space Administration
NHS	National Health Service
OLAs	operating level agreements
PACSI	perform, accountable, control, suggest, inform
PESTEL	political, economic, social, technological, environmental, legal
RACI	responsible, accountable, consulted, informed
SLA	service level agreement
SMART	specific, measurable, accurate, reliable, time
SME	small medium enterprise
SWOT	strengths, weaknesses, opportunities, threats
TSPM	target, scale, plan, measure

1 Introduction to the six-stage general model of business partnering

Introduction – the act of beginning something new

The whole is greater than the sum of its parts.

Aristotle

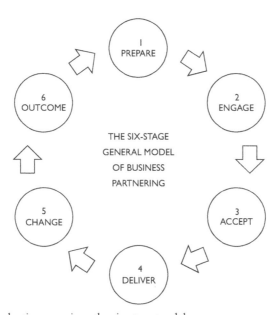

Figure 1.1 Introduction overview: the six-stage model

This chapter provides the context of business partnering and an explanation of the stages of the general model of business partnering.

Knowledge components considered within this chapter

What is it?

- introduction
- context and scope
- historical and current context
- definitions of stakeholders and business partners.

Why do it?

- why business partnering is important
- the three key approaches: control, service, or advisory
- the overview of the lifecycle stages of a business partner.

WHAT IS IT?

Introduction

The key outcomes for this book will be to support:

1 individuals who wish to gain a comprehensive understanding of business partnering;
2 a new business partner who does not have the requisite knowledge;
3 an existing business partner who has identified potential gaps in knowledge and skills which should be improved or applied;
4 the business partner's line managers;
5 stakeholders engaging with business partners;
6 functional business leaders who wish to improve their business partnering outcomes;
7 functional business leaders who are considering establishing a business partnering program.

In all of the these cases, increasing knowledge and skills will support the resulting outcome of increased applied competence.

Context and scope

The context of the general partnering model will apply to individuals who are working in organizations, whether profitmaking or not-for-profit.

The scope includes:

- a general model for business partnering for the individual;
- the model applies to both for-profit and not-for-profit organizations, the term business partnering can apply to both;
- a model based on six stages.

The six stages of the general model are:

The preparation stage (Chapter 2)

Chapter 2 will outline the initial preparation required by the business partner, the teams that they must engage with, and engagement with the organization as a whole.

The initial individual preparation process should support the self-review of the skills, knowledge and competences that may be required. Self-review, or self-assessment is the process of evaluation of one's skills, capabilities, attitudes and performance. This is the starting point of efficient preparation. This self-insight will help to support the initial assessment of what the stakeholder power base might be, to assess the stakeholder's team's needs, and to assess the style that may be the most appropriate to adopt. The requirements of the business partnership relationship can therefore be developed and then established from an initial firm foundation of understanding that will support a strong bonding or 'contract' with their stakeholders. This will support the organizational outcomes.

The engagement stage (Chapter 3)

The engagement stage establishes the engagement process, service content and emotional contract with the stakeholders. The engagement process is a method, and should be on-going rather than a single occurrence; the initial engagement is critical to developing an effective long-term relationship. The service content is framed by two simple boundaries. What are the technical demands required from your partner and what you can supply as a business partner. The emotional contract includes the attitudes, beliefs, perceptions and trust that both parties will share with each other. A significant overlap of the concepts behind the context will support the establishment of a contract based on trust. This tends to operate at a subconscious level between both parties.

The acceptance stage (Chapter 4)

This includes the management of conflict, acceptance and integration issues that business partners face. Although there may be a firm agreement from the outset of the relationship, conflicts will occur due to a variety of factors and these will be explored in more detail within Chapter 4. Acceptance occurs when both parties share common aims, objectives and goals that they wish to achieve together. These are bound by a condition of mutual satisfaction by both parties. Integration is the degree in which the aims, objectives and goals are unified and assimilated.

The delivery stage (Chapter 5)

This includes the review of business, delivery and operating models that can be applied. It defines the type of delivery that includes goals, aims, targets, outcomes, outputs and objectives including the constraints and enablers that may apply. Within these delivery types a variety of potential delivery models are then considered. These vary from strategic goals to individual and team objectives. The fundamental paradigm for the business partner is their value proposition and contribution towards effective delivery of organizational operations.

The change stage (Chapter 6)

This includes the review of strategic, tactical and operational drivers that dominate change. Strategies of dealing with resistance and supporting positive engagement are explored. Change is powered by strategic, tactical, and operational causes; these impact on the attainment of the change requirement being pursued. Applying the optimum change model(s) will enhance success and mitigate the risks of failure. Change is to move from an old state to a new state. What causes and drives changes, what resistance might be expected, and how to overcome them are reviewed. More positively, the enablers of positive and successful change are defined and explored with the relevant methodologies that can be applied.

The outcome stage (Chapter 7)

The personal outcomes for the business partner are interrelated with the stakeholder, their teams and the organizational outcomes. The outcomes of any operating model will impact the personal outcomes for the business partner and these will include their own financial and non-financial rewards. Additionally the business partner's personal development, trust and their ethical standards will have been enhanced. The alignment of these to those of the stakeholder and their teams towards organizational alignment creates a powerful line of sight for the outcomes being aimed for or targeted. The review of how the knowledge, skills and competences relate to current and new operating models is considered. In addition the entity outcomes that relate to organizational, stakeholder and team expectations of the outcomes to be delivered are reviewed.

The general model, by definition, is not functionally or organizationally based. However, the discussion will refer to case studies and examples where they can provide deeper understanding.

Historical and current context

The emergence of added value for partnering

The business partner concept emphasizes a move towards added value teamwork and specialization, rather than focusing on a range of diverse general skills and

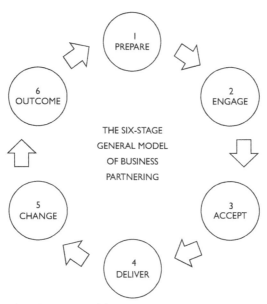

Figure 1.2 Explanation six-stage model overview

requirements of multiple interested parties. Yet, if we reach back in time where does the concept of specialization of activities occur?

Aristotle lived in ancient Greece from 384–322 BCE. His writings covered many different subjects and are the source of many well-known quotes, one of which is used in business 'the whole is greater than the sum of the parts'. Teamwork between partners can deliver much greater outcomes than an individual can. This is an emerging argument for the concept of added value.

The emergence of specialization

Adam Smith in his book *The Wealth of Nations* (1776) defines the causes of improvement in the productive powers of labour. This has been a driver for wealth creation for nations. The growth of business partnering has been driven by many organizations that need to achieve improvements. There is still current relevance today from Smith's historical work in relation to business partnering.

The key elements of how it relates to the growth of business partnering are:

The division of labour

Division of labour has been one of the great drivers of increasing productivity. This is based on:

- improving the knowledge, skill, and experience of staff to increase the quantity of the work they can perform;

- reducing staff activities to core operations, and making these operations the sole focus will increase productivity;
- creating a sensible balance of how much experienced staff is supported with by applying the proper processes.

The specialization of labour

Specialization of labour will:

- increase the competences and skills of the individual;
- improve co-operation by using the sum of everyone's talent, which in turn will increase productivity.

The division of labour is limited by size

The context for business partnering are:

- smaller organizations have less opportunity to specialize labour than larger ones;
- larger organizations drive technological innovation by giving intense focus to certain tasks, and allowing staff to brainstorm ways to make these tasks more productive; this, again, adds to increased efficiency.

The emergence of the 'business partner' in current times

The business partner concept was initially used by Ulrich (1996). He identified the requirement that HR. change from its traditional and core roles of administration to being more proactive and strategic in its outlook.

He identified four roles that HR should deliver concurrently:

1   The 'strategic partner' role is process-orientated and focuses on the future strategic management of employees and the alignment of the function with business strategy.
2   The 'administrative expert' role is primarily concerned with dealing with day-to-day operational matters. The focus is on achieving operational efficiency through improving work processes, e.g. the introduction of shared services.
3   The 'employee champion' role reflects the responsibility of functional practitioners to listen and respond to the expressed needs of employees.
4   The final role is that of 'change agent' with an emphasis on building the capacity of the organization to embrace change and transformation.

(Raja *et al.*, 2010)

Different functions have developed by increasing their professionalism to the skill, knowledge and competences that they apply. These are based on a variety of factors that include:

- exercising legitimate control on activities;
- creating barriers of entry by the placement of technical standards;
- independent ethical standards;
- seeking power and influence upon the organization;
- formal accreditation or certification of their expertise.

In these cases, the autonomy and authority of the group relates to its power and status within the business organization, that is, 'to be numbered amongst the controllers rather than the controlled'. However, to be successful in achieving such authority, these specialisms not only need to identify a key business problem and highlight how their expertise alone can solve it, but in addition they must maintain control over their expertise and prevent rivals from usurping or annexing their knowledge. Importantly, issues of professional ethics and altruism appear less central in attaining organizational autonomy and authority, although such themes are often stressed within the professional associations that develop around such managerial specialisms.

(Wright 2010)

Several professions have been more effective in attaining greater prominence within their organisations. However traditional boundaries are becoming blurred. The drivers of this include:

- structural reorganisations;
- increased emphasis of end-to-end processes and activities that span across all functions;
- technology;
- emergence of new occupational groups;
- professional bodies increasing the boundaries that they might serve.

In addition to the professional push and the internal organizational pull towards more efficiency, there has been a drive towards business partnering from outside trends, that demand increased effectiveness. Some examples include:

- the advent and development of shared services;
- the shrinking and repositioning of functions due to cost pressures;
- a drive to have more empowered staff;
- the trend towards self-service, agile working and flexible working because of improvements in technology.

A more holistic approach to business partnering is outlined below:

The following is as applicable to business partnering as to classic personal relationships: to fulfil your role as a partner, you have to pay attention to the requirements, needs and conditions of the other party in the relationship.

The trust principle demands that you must prove yourself to be basically fair in order to be accepted as a long-term reliable partner.

(Wucherer, 2006)

Definitions of stakeholders and business partners

Stakeholders

The definition of stakeholders and their scope and context are less problematical in relation to any functional perspective and have more commonality and acceptance of understanding. A stakeholder who can be inside or outside an organization may have some of these common attributes:

- persons, groups or organizations who are engaged by leaders, managers and business partners of an organization;
- any individual or group who can affect or is affected by the achievement of the organization's objectives;
- any individual or business function that controls elements of the organization's resources, services or processes that are being provided and relied upon;
- individuals with power and influence who can significantly affect any strategic changes for the organization they work with or within.

They can relate to profit and non-profit organizations, and can be inside or outside the organization e.g. service provision.

My working definition of stakeholders in this book will be:

A stakeholder is an individual or group, either within or outside an organization that has an interest in the services, outputs or outcomes being provided to them and which they also have influence or power over.

These attributes and this definition of stakeholders will used throughout the following chapters.

Business partner

There are many different definitions of business partnering because of differences in perspectives, use and application. However, there are several common features that will support effective business partnering. These include:

1   the ability to co-operate with each stakeholder under conditions where there is weak alignment;
2   acceptance that all goals and objectives will not always be perfectly aligned;
3   where there is a perceived breach of trust, this is addressed constructively and remedied;

4   agreement about 'who is doing what' in the relation to business change or organizational changes;

5   recognition of any shortfall in skill and beginning a process of addressing any gap;

6   having appropriate conflict resolution processes in place;

7   having an open and empathetic approach between team members.

There is currently no universally acknowledged definition for business partnering. This has not prevented functions from adopting it, thereby increasing legitimacy of its use within the context that they operate in. The use of 'business' in conjunction with 'partnering' could in itself be misleading, for example, what if the business is a social enterprise or charitable organization? For consistency, in this book the term 'business partnering', will apply to both for-profit and not-for profit organizations.

My working definition of business partnering in this book will be:

> An effective business partner is an individual who can add value within a team through their specialisms, skills, knowledge, competences, and experiences to deliver greater organizational outcomes.

Effective business partnering should include these paradigms:

1   to seek win–win solutions with stakeholders and have common objectives;

2   that both parties mutually support the shared goals and objectives;

3   that the relationship is based on and developed with mutual trust;

4   to support change, which is being driven by economic, technological, organizational, or marketplace changes;

5   to apply the skills, knowledge, and competences required in the partnering relationship;

6   to have in place effective governance and ethics so that both parties share mutual respect.

This definition and the above paradigms will be used throughout the following chapters rather than being myopically bound by any strict narrow functional definition(s), examples of these will be examined within the following section.

Functional perspectives

My working definition of function in this book will be:

> Individuals, groups or teams that are assigned with specific responsibilities and accountabilities to maintain control and deliver outcomes within a defined and agreed scope.

A few specific examples of functions include:

- finance
- human resources (HR)
- information technology (IT)
- procurement.

How these relate to business partnering are examined later in this chapter.

All organizations carry out a level of business partnering to support their core business activities and processes. Business partnering can include support for its own business functions, for example, finance, human resources, IT, or procurement. It can also include support for other functions and could also include activities and processes outside the core organization, for example, to external customers and suppliers.

The legitimacy of business partnering depends upon the context, maturity, scope and focus and intention of the relationships of:

1   the individual business partnership relationships to various functions, e.g. finance within a business unit;
2   the relationship of business partnering between functions within an organization, e.g. HR with IT;
3   the relationship and degree of relationship with external organizations, e.g. procurement with suppliers.

Emerging definitions that are legitimizing the use of business partnering

The legitimization of the use of business partnering, context and definitions include:

The human resources perspective

WHAT IS HR BUSINESS PARTNERING?

> HR business partnering is a model whereby HR professionals work closely with business leaders and/or line managers to achieve shared organizational objectives, in particular designing and implementing HR systems and processes that support strategic business aims. This can involve the formal designation of 'HR business partners' – HR professionals who are embedded within specific areas of the business. Many varying definitions of HR business partnering exist and the role of HR business partners can vary widely from one organization to another.
>
> (CIPD, 2005)

THE HR CONTEXT

To improve the status and added value proposition to the organization a trend has developed within HR for the role of business partner to be promoted and implemented. HR managers interpret business partnering as a new role. However there are still open issues and questions that might apply:

- What is the extent of the use of the business partner concept?
- What is the scope of responsibilities and accountabilities?
- Do the business partners operate within HR, or are they placed within the teams they support?
- How does this impact upon the efficiency of the HR function?
- What is the true added value impact upon the effectiveness of the organisational outcomes?

This has impacts in three ways. First, does the split of strategic transformational activities from transactional support weaken the cohesiveness within the function? Second, does this inadvertently reduce the collaboration between the two groups as they compete for resources? Third, does it allow for rival professions or managerial groups to become business partners within HR, for example, functions or subsidiaries within which an organization might wish to control talent management, remuneration, recruitment and training decisions independently using an inhouse or outsource service provider? Yet the human resource strategy remains within HR.

The finance perspective

WHAT IS FINANCE BUSINESS PARTNERING?

In effect the function needs to influence business outcomes rather than report upon business results.

> Finance business partnering is an extension of the financial director's role as a trusted advisor. Finance must take on a new role as a financial coach to the business. Many chief financial officers (CFOs) may have long 'partnered' with chief executive officers (CEOs) to perform this role at that strategic level. The current development is for finance personnel to take on new roles as finance business partners, supporting decision making throughout the business, as players on the business team rather than scorekeepers on the side line.
>
> (CIMA, 2009: 15)

THE FINANCE CONTEXT

Within their organizations finance will still need to focus on their traditional focus on:

- accounting processes
- financial and statutory reporting

- budgeting and forecasting
- risk management
- tax compliance
- management accounting and analysis.

The requirement for change management skills to influence organizational outcomes have been recognized for decades. Yet the focus of many finance functions has been upon reducing their cost base as opposed to enhancing enterprise value with the knowledge, competences and skills that finance can apply. The trend is now moving from the perception of finance as being a cost for the organisation to a function that positively impacts organisational outcomes. This has been the catalyst for the increasing adoption of the business partner within the function. Innovative organisations are now deploying business partners to support and impact organisational outcomes. These early adopters may already have finance employees with business partners in their job title as opposed to the traditional finance manager title. The increasing global trend is to enhance management accounting and analysis, and this supports the increasing deployment of business partners.

The procurement perspective

WHAT IS PROCUREMENT BUSINESS PARTNERING?

A primary requirement for procurement is that everyone is part of the supply chain. This may seem a simplistic approach that requires all functions to part of the same end-to-end process, yet in practice it is complex and with the deployment of technologies can become very sophisticated. Business partners will, in the main, be deployed to support internal stakeholders or external suppliers.

THE PROCUREMENT CONTEXT

The context for business partnering in procurement can be described as follows:

> Procurement's journey from transactional processing to strategic business partnering is not fully complete. Some personal successes are evident, but they are individual achievements, not an organizational model that can be copied. We argue that this should surprise no one. There are too many unresolved conflicts between the role of procurement and its internal clients. Where good relationships exist, they do so between individuals who trust each other in spite of these conflicts. It is argued that trust is fundamental and essential in the type of relationship that procurement is aiming for, but that the metrics and governance used by procurement are antithetical to its aims. A genuine understanding of and concern for clients' ambitions and goals is needed.

The management of suppliers includes many facets from price negotiations, performance evaluation, and risk analysis all the way down to innovation and collaboration management.

(Young and Green, 2011)

The drive to evolve business partnering within procurement will remain a significant challenge where traditional metrics and adversarial commercial negotiations are prevalent. Where the relationship is more collaborative in nature, seeking mutual 'win–win' outcomes for both parties then the business partnering relationship is likely to be positively developed and mutually supported.

The information technology perspective

WHAT IS INFORMATION TECHNOLOGY PARTNERING?

Business partnering embodies a set of competencies, knowledge, skills, and behaviours that foster a productive, value-producing relationship between the IT function to other functions within an organization for example HR, IT, finance, legal, and also to other external providers. These competences can be leveraged through organizational roles, a discipline, and an organizational capability.

BUSINESS PARTNER CHALLENGES

Chief information officers (CIO) need to be aware of the business requirement to improve performance between IT and the organisation.

The best business strategies are informed by the possibilities of how technology can provide new sources of competitive advantage. Business leaders often fail to articulate business needs in a way that IT can actually implement. In some cases, business partners cannot articulate their needs or do not articulate them with enough lead-time. Even when partners can express their needs, they may use language that forces IT into a corner by requesting systems or functionality, rather than by definition of business requirements and capabilities.

(Shah, 2011)

Improvements can be achieved by:

- building streamlined support to end-users;
- changing or improving the stakeholder operating model by the use of technology;
- providing the required skills.

Summary

In summary, there are different professional perspectives and definitions by various functions that have legitimized their own perspective and use. Although they have different functional context and application. The initial examples of functional business partnering definitions are not definitive within these functions nor are they universal in their application. In addition to this there can also be a degree of variability of use within the organization and this will be influenced on their business requirements, state of evolution and culture either corporately or within their countries. The deployment, use, scope and definition of business partnering applies to a much wider base of essential business relationships, for example legal services, outsourcing activities within functions and organizational business to business partnering arrangements.

This book will focus on the end-to-end process of how an individual can become an efficient and effective business partner in any professional environment. The model that will be examined is not bound by any specific functional or enterprise definitions or constraints. It provides a new partnering model that can be applied generically and in-depth to all functions and organizations.

WHY DO IT?

Why business partnering is important

Effective business partnering is important at three connected levels, the:

- individual
- functional/team
- organizational.

The emphasis of the following chapters is upon the individual skills, knowledge and competences that can be applied. However, an understanding and appreciation of the partnering process at an enterprise and cross-functional level will facilitate enhanced delivery of organizational outcomes.

Why is it important at an individual level?

The context at the individual level of business partnering is the focus upon the relationships within the teams they operate in.

The potential benefits of effective business partnering for an individual within that role include:

- better alignment of personal and business goals;
- improved job enrichment;
- increased scope of responsibilities.

- better promotional prospects;
- improved personal connections within and outside the organization;
- improved personal satisfaction;
- enhanced skills, knowledge and competences;
- the potential for higher salary;
- being more marketable both internally and externally.

Why is it important at a functional level?

At a functional level, business partnering will be dependent on organizational requirements and circumstances and, should initially focus upon its relationship and activities with other functions, for example human resources with finance, IT with procurement, and so on.

The benefits and justification of effective functional business partnering include:

- collaborative decision-making;
- influencing future performance;
- the development of aligned functional targets, goals and objectives;
- improved teamwork, including across functions;
- improves cross-fertilization of ideas;
- staff development, by attracting and retaining the best talent;
- collaborative styles of working;
- creating common ways of working for internal stakeholders;
- developing better 'trade-offs' on activities;
- developing and improving end-to-end processes;
- reducing costs and improving cashflows;
- improving cycle times;
- joint enhancement of the customer service experience;
- improved outcomes for the organization.

Why is it important at an enterprise level?

At the enterprise level, the context for business partnering will, in the main, focus upon external stakeholders, including suppliers and customers.

The benefits of effective enterprise business partnering include:

- increased customer satisfaction;
- better value for the client;
- recognition and protection of profit margin for contractors and suppliers;
- staff development and satisfaction;
- creation of an environment that encourages and technical development;
- understanding between partners and driving down of real costs;
- design integration with specialists in the supply chain through early involvement of the contractors;

- better predictability of time and cost, and overall delivery period;
- stability that provides more confidence for better planning and investment in staff and resources.

(Constructing Excellence, 2004)

It is essential that an effective business partner has a good working knowledge of the key individuals, team and organizational issues that support the linkage to goals and outcome delivery requirements.

The three key approaches: advisory, service or control

As explored in the previous section, efficient individual partnering may not be undertaken separately from the functional and enterprise influences. The organizational requirements and the markets or stakeholders they need to serve will determine the style and context of the individual business partnering.

There are three broad styles that are likely to be set from corporate goals and culture. These are:

1 advisory
2 service
3 control.

The advisory style for business partnering

The advisory style is likely to have the following features and attributes.
These will be focused at a strategic level, for example long-term requirements.

- The business partner will support the customer or stakeholder requirements by giving specialist advice.
- They will not be a part of the team, however they will guide on opportunities, restrictions and risks.
- Their activities will be based on enterprise outcomes.
- The stakeholders they serve are likely to have no impact upon the remuneration and rewards of the business partner.
- The service levels will be based on a specific requirement, or issues.
- Comparisons between teams are, broadly, irrelevant.

The advisory style will align to the governance model of organization to organization business partnering.

The service style for business partnering

The service style is likely to have the following features and attributes.
They will focus at a tactical level, for example, medium-term requirements.

- The business partner will support the customer or stakeholder service requirements.
- They will be part of the team in which they operate.
- Their activities will be based on the routine activities of their partnership.
- The stakeholders they serve will impact the remuneration and rewards of the business partner.
- The service levels will be unique to the teams that they operate within.
- A comparison between teams is unimportant.

The service style will align to the intra-organizational partnering model.

The control style for business partnering

The control style is likely to have the following features and attributes. They will be in the main at an operating level:

- The business partner will be based within the function that they specialize in.
- The goals and objectives will be set centrally.
- Service levels will be based on targets.
- The remuneration and rewards will be established by the function.
- The level of standardization required is important.
- Compliance to the rules and policies is critical.
- This model supports comparisons across business partnering activities.

The control style will align to the intra-organizational partnering model.

Each of the three broad approaches will be successful within different organizations. Which approach is likely to be adopted will be dependent on the following attributes:

- the culture of the organization;
- the style of the chief executive and the board;
- the degree of centralized or decentralized decision-making;
- the situation that the organization faces in the short, medium and long term;
- the power requirements at board level;
- the business environment in which the organization operates.

The broad contrasts of the different styles are compared in the template in Table 1.1.

As outlined above there is no specific approach that fits all organization requirements, and it may be possible for all three styles to be embedded within an organization.

In practice the approaches and attributes are likely to be ambiguous and the styles and attributes of the business partner change over time. However, having awareness of the main approaches and attributes will help to provide a business partnering business model to be initially developed.

Table 1.1 Advisory, service and control styles of business partnering

	Advisory	*Service*	*Control*
Focus	Strategic outcomes	Tactical outputs	Operational inputs
Cultures	Consensus-based	Bottom-up listening	Top-down instructions
Style	Laissez faire	Empowering	Autocratic
Power styles	No goals are set; expert power	Goals are driven bottom-up; reward power	Goals are set top-down; coercive power
Level of centralization	Matrix style	Decentralized	Central
Organizational situation	Risks and opportunities are in balance and neutral	Market opportunities exist	Risks are significant
Power requirements	Interpretation of the policies is provided	Broad guidelines are in place	Rules are to be complied with
Potential governance alignment	Organizational to organizational	Intra organizational	Functional business partnering

The paradigms and paradoxes of the general model

There are several key paradigms that will clarify and define the life cycle of business partnering.

The paradigms for the model

1   The model applies to both for-profit and not-for profit organizations.
2   Businesses and organizations may have different objectives or outcomes, however the processes within them are similar.
3   There are six distinct stages of the general model that can be efficiently and effectively applied to business partnering.
4   The general model is iterative rather than a single cycle of the six stages.
5   The six stages relate to each other and are aligned within an end-to-end cycle.
6   The greater the engagement and two-way constructive feedback between business partners and stakeholders, the more dynamic the relationship will be.

The paradoxes for the model

There are paradoxes that may relate to the model. These are:

•   The initial engagement and continuing application of business partnering may vary both within an organization and a function.

- The business partner may be placed within any of the six stages inside the partnering cycle.
- The entry and exit point within the partnering cycle will determine the efficiency and effectiveness of the partnering relationship.
- The business partner may have been placed or promoted into a role and their skills, knowledge and competences are diffused across all six stages of the model.

Chapter summary

The general business model applies to the six life cycle stages to business partnering. There are different approaches and styles for business partnering. The styles are categorized as: advisory, service and control. It reviews the different professional functions perspectives that can be applied. This chapter explains the importance of business partnering for the individual, function and at an organizational level.

Chapter 2 now follows which is the first stage of the general model. This outlines the dimensions of individual, team, and organizational preparedness.

References

CIMA (2009). *Improving Decision Making in Organizations: The Opportunity to Reinvent Finance Business Partners*, London: CIMA. Retrieved 8 March 2015 from http://www.cimaglobal. com/Documents/Thought_leadership_docs/cid_execrep_finance_business_partners_ Jul09.pdf

CIPD (2015). 'Factsheet HR business partnering' Retrieved 11 November 2015 from http://www.cipd.co.uk/hr-resources/factsheets/hr-business-partnering.aspx

Constructing Excellence (2004) 'Partnering Factsheet'. Retrieved 26 November 2015 from http://constructingexcellence.org.uk/wp-content/uploads/2015/03/partnering.pdf

Raja, J. Z., Green, S. D. & Leiringer, R. (2010). 'Concurrent and disconnected change programmes: strategies in support of servitization and the implementation of business partnering'. *Human Resource Management Journal* 20(3): 258–276.

Shah, S.(2011).'Perfecting the IT-business partnership'. *Baseline*. Retrieved 8 March 2015 from http://www.baselinemag.com/c/a/IT-Management/Perfecting-the-ITBusiness-Partnership-330416/#sthash.89UIXT0Q.pdf

Smith, A. (1798). *An Enquiry into the Nature and Causes of the Wealth of Nations*. 5th edn. London: Methuen & Co.

Ulrich, D. (1996) *Human Resource Champions: The Next Agenda for Adding Value and Delivering Results*. Cambridge, MA: Harvard Business School Press.

Wright, C. (2008). 'Reinventing human resource management: Business partners, internal consultants and the limits to professionalization'. *Human Relations*, 61(8): 1063–1086.

Wucherer, K. (2006) 'Business partnering: a driving force for innovation', *Industrial Marketing Management*, 35(1): 91–102.

Young, B. & Green, C. H. (2011). 'The role of procurement as trusted advisor to management'. Retrieved 8 March 2015 from http://trustedadvisor.com/articles/the-role-of-procurement-as-trusted-advisor-to-management

2 Preparation – the first stage

Prepare: To make something ready for use or consideration.

(Oxford Dictionaries Online)

Success depends upon previous preparation, and without such preparation there is sure to be failure.

(Confucius)

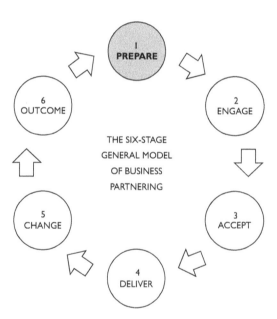

Figure 2.1 Preparation overview

This chapter considers the initial preparations required for individual, team, and organization business partnering engagement.

Knowledge components considered within this chapter

Individual preparation

- self-learning and responsibility
- the initial induction process.

Preparing for team engagement

- the power of the stakeholder
- personal and stakeholder team assessments
- the different styles of business partnering.

Preparing for the engagement with the organization

- appraising the culture of the organization
- the initial organizational situational appraisal
- the impact and priority matrix.

INDIVIDUAL PREPARATION

The requirement for the personal responsibility for self-learning and induction is outlined. The power of the stakeholder and how this impacts other stakeholders and teams will influence the style that should be adopted by the business partner. The organizational culture and current situation determines the priorities that the business partner should prepare for and then focus on.

This chapter reviews the preparation that the business partner should consider, ranging from an individual micro review to a macro or big picture review of the organization and the markets it operates within. A broad understanding will help support answering these open questions that the business partner may face:

- How do I undertake an assessment of my skills and readiness?
- What is the range of dimensions that I should consider?
- What might the stakeholder requirements be?
- How will I relate to the teams that I will support and operate within?
- What types of styles for business partnering would be best?

The three sections in this chapter include self-preparation by the business partner, preparation for the teams that they will operate in, and the organizational culture, situations and functions that they will be engaging with, for example finance, HR, IT or procurement.

Self-learning and responsibility

The lines of enquiry mentioned above are initial examples and starting points to commence the business partnering dimensions that need to be understood, it is also insufficient to have a single skill-set. Skills need to be enhanced and, to stay up to date and relevant. Consequently new business partners are likely to be assessed according to for their ability for self-development as well for their current skills. Organizations that support the principles of continuous skills acquisition for their staff will be more successful in achieving their goals and retaining high-performing staff. Conversely, some organizations simply do not acknowledge the importance and significance of their investment in training for their goals and the motivational impact upon staff. Learning whilst performing the requirements of the position has always been an implicit norm and will continue to be prevalent. Nevertheless, continual learning and acquisition of knowledge, skills and competences are of great importance. The business partner should not just rely upon what the organization provides, they should also rely upon themselves.

Knowledge

Knowledge can be divided into three types:

- personal knowledge
- procedural knowledge
- propositional knowledge.

These three knowledge attributes should be assimilated by an effective business partner as they will support effective stakeholder and organizational outcomes. However, knowledge without linking commonalties (skill) or creating new insights (competences) may be insufficient to meet stakeholder needs and requirements.

Figure 2.2 has no axis – it simply demonstrates knowledge as individual elements that have yet to be related to each other. There are no commonalties, the knowledge sets are in isolation from one another.

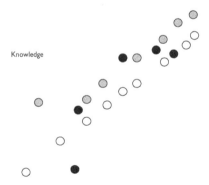

Figure 2.2 Knowledge

Personal knowledge

The personal knowledge base will be initially dependent on the education and professional training of the individual business partner.

For example, this could include:

- first degree
- MBA and other master's degree
- professional body accreditation within their functional specialisms
- PhD.

These form an initial degree and depth of learning, which will support efficient business partnering, however depth of knowledge is questionable in the future for its completeness and effectiveness. As outlined in Chapter 1 there are different biases from professional bodies. This bias is based on their professional 'lens' and how they relate to their business partners from a functional perspective.

Procedural knowledge

Procedural knowledge will be primarily based on working within the organization. Some examples of high-level procedural knowledge include: IT security issues, financial procedures, human resource rules and regulations, and procurement methods. Within an organization, procedural knowledge, in practice, will required to be operated at a more detailed level which is particular to that organization's governance, culture and business goals and outcome requirements.

Propositional knowledge

Propositional knowledge is based on the facts that the business partner and their stakeholder can believe, assimilate and then jointly act upon.

The use of facts should enable the following:

- to keep the business partner stakeholders aligned towards the organizational targets, goals or objectives;
- to facilitate addressing existing, emerging and new opportunities;
- to build trust and confidence with each other;
- to include the business partner and stakeholders in effective decision making;
- to assign clear roles and responsibilities for who, what and how action is taken;
- to include the competences and collective knowledge of all the stakeholders;
- to facilitate the use of information in an open, accurate and timely manner.

Case study: knowledge

This case study relates to technical knowledge in isolation, without social skills and competences being in place. How effective is business partnering without social skills?

THE CONTEXT OF THE CASE STUDY

- The business partner was working within engineering on a decentralized basis, and was recently promoted to a middle management position.
- He was studying for an MBA at a leading business school with emphasis on personal development.
- The enterprise was a large multinational.
- The individual had a very high IQ.
- This was a discussion within the MBA personal development programme in their tutorial group.

WHAT OCCURRED

The engineering business partner was newly promoted and this was the discussion between him (BP) and his tutorial group (TG):

BP: Its great, I have just got a new promotion.
TG: That's fantastic, well done, why did they promote you?
BP: Due to my technical knowledge and skills to support the rest of the team.
TG: Are you enjoying it?
BP: In the main, yes I have new responsibilities, better pay and bonuses … there is one thing though …
TG: What is that then?
BP: I am in an open office with all the team.
TG: How are you dealing with it then?
BP: Simple really, I have placed my desk against a wall, so I face the wall, I can get on with my own work and then there is no requirement to speak to anyone when I am busy.

KEY POINTS

1 The individual had significant business knowledge and technical skills.
2 The basic competence of social interaction was severely lacking.
3 Technical expertise is not the same as being a competent business partner.
4 The individual had no self-awareness of the impact his behaviours were having on the team.
5 In essence technical knowledge is a small part of the requirements for effective stakeholder engagement.

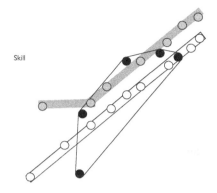

Skill

Figure 2.3 Skill

Skills

A skill can be simply defined as doing something well based on the knowledge that has already been assimilated.

Figure 2.3 illustrates that skills link to the individual commonalities of knowledge elements.

There are three features that can be applied to effective business relationships; these are hard, soft, and partnering skills.

Hard skills are quantifiable and can be measured. These will be acquired through education, learning, professional bodies and practical experiences.

Soft skills are personality driven and individually based, these, for example, include social cohesion, level of optimism, and interaction with other team members. The use of relevant soft skills can create better outcomes for the organization.

Partnering skills are the core requirements for effective engagement. Softer non-technical skills will deepen the engagement with the stakeholder. These include:

- *Active listening:* the ability to provide full and complete attention, comprehend the opinions being made, not interrupting and seeking points of clarification when required.
- *Critical thinking;* this is the use of cognitive thoughts to identify the insights, options, and opportunities in relation to potential outcomes.
- *Analytical analysis:* this is the evaluation of data from multiple sources, the development of information, and evidence collation, towards the implementation of joint solutions that deliver agreed outcomes.
- *Decision making:* this is considering both the qualitative and quantitative information that is available to the business partner and their stakeholders.

Figure 2.4 Competence

Competence

Competences can be defined as the application of knowledge and skills in a variety of different and complex situations. Figure 2.4 demonstrates that competences link knowledge in new and innovative ways beyond the skill level.

As outlined in Chapter 1, several professional bodies have legitimized business partnering from their own perspectives. Complete reliance on any professional training is likely to fall short of the full requirements for efficient and effective business partnering. Business partnering capabilities and competences will support the development of efficient and effective business partnering that focus upon stakeholder and organizational outcomes. Competences will lead to the development of capabilities for more senior roles within an organization. Examples of the development link between business partner competences and future leadership capabilities are shown in Table 2.1.

An effective business partner induction program will support the rapid assimilation of knowledge, skills and competences. An organizational structured competence framework would also support this.

The initial induction process

The induction process outlined below applies to a new business partner or employee who is new to the organization. However where the business partner is already a part of the organization or has an incomplete understanding of the stakeholder there may be elements of self-gathering of information to close any knowledge gaps. Regardless of this, one of the key expectations from the stakeholder is that knowledge of the business partner is comprehensive and complete.

For an individual to commence business partnering there is a level of basic knowledge and understanding of the business or organization that needs to be assimilated. This is normally provided through an induction programme. Induction is a process where employees adjust to or familiarize themselves with their jobs and the working environment, and every organization, large or

Table 2.1 Business partner competences

Leadership capability
- respecting the diversity of opinions and experiences
- supporting constructive behaviours
- establishing rules of engagement in relation to conflict and decisions

Excellent and exemplar leadership qualities
- appreciating market drivers
- understanding the value of chain on the market and where the organization creates added value
- understanding of the organizational operating model
- having functional expertise that can be applied and supported in business partnering relationships
- having detailed stakeholder knowledge

Business knowledge that create insights for new products and markets
- focusing on outcome-based solutions
- meeting quality standards
- respecting time targets
- ensuring specifications and scope are respected
- having change management skills

Project implementations that constantly succeed in meeting their objectives
- working to agreed rules of engagement
- giving and providing respect
- working as a system rather than a collection of individuals.

Building great teamwork
- supporting the team
- acknowledging positive behaviours
- diminishing negative behaviours
- having positive relationship skills

Individual and team mentoring and coaching
- giving clear and concise messages
- having consistency
- understanding the culture of the business and stakeholders within it

Brilliant communication skills
- developing camaraderie
- creating and supporting an environment of trust
- interacting constructively
- respecting differences in culture
- sowing optimism

Behavioural standards and ethics that are exemplar for the organization
- having empathy with the pressures that your business partners are experiencing
- recognizing the degree of change or level stability that that is in place
- understanding the organizational targets and outcomes that are required

small, should have a professionally structured induction program. The business partner's line manager will normally be responsible for the induction process. However, it may be delegated to other functions and managers. The induction process will vary between organizations and also in its consistent application within an organization.

An example of a well defined organizational induction program and the roles and activities are:

Line manager roles and activities

1   They should explain how the team operates, the obligations of the role, expectations of management and the business partner's key stakeholders, the terms and requirements for any probationary period;
2   an overview of the organization's history, current strategy and objectives, products and services, and culture;
3   an overview of the performance management system and incentive programmes;
4   introduction to the key members to the organization is a fundamental activity. Ideally the exiting post holder should be included as part of that handover. Planning for these activities in advance are important;
5   a personal introduction to their fellow team members;
6   provide and explain day-to-day guidance in local procedures.

Human resources

1   To provide a comfortable introduction for the employee to the organization;
2   to brief them of relevant HR support, for example available learning, training and development services.

If an effective induction programme is not in place, then the above will provide a framework and checklist to assimilate the basic factors that should be integrated. New employee orientation programmes have been shown to socialize newcomers and increase their knowledge, skills, and abilities when completed. These types of programmes are perhaps the most influential piece of an employee's development (Aceveda and Yancey, 2011). The induction programme will not normally include professional competences, as there would be an expectation that the business partner has already acquired this knowledge base. Ethical threats and governance safeguards can be overlooked in an induction programme, and are a key organization leadership requirement and capability.

PREPARING FOR TEAM ENGAGEMENT

The power of the stakeholder will influence how the business partner will engage with them and their teams. It will support:

- the application of the optimum management style adopted by the business partner;
- the development of mutual trust;
- the engagement process with their teams;
- the impact and priorities that are being required or targeted.

Power of the stakeholder

The assessment of the power of the stakeholder and how the business partner should relate to this should be a significant initial consideration.

A prominent examination on the power that may be also applied in the context of business partnering and stakeholders was by John French and Bertram Raven (Raven 1965).

They initially identified five bases of power:

- personal
- referent
- legitimate
- reward
- coercive.

And then, latterly, a sixth power base was identified: Information power

The business partner relationship with their stakeholder will be dependent on respecting each others power. The business partner will have personal power and the stakeholder will have positional power (Table 2.2).

The power of the business partner in relation to the stakeholder

Expert power

Expert power, in relation to the business partner's power position, will be based on the more significant competences they have in specialisms that can then be applied. They will have acquired the relevant knowledge, skills and competences that empower them to analyse specific circumstances, and forward options or recommendations. Stakeholders will acknowledge and generally

Table 2.2 Power balance

Business partner	Stakeholder
The power balance between the business partner and stakeholder	
Expert power	Legitimate power
Referent power	Reward power
Information power	Coercive power

support the recommendations being made. When expertise is demonstrated, stakeholders will trust and respect what the business partner's opinions are. As a subject matter expert, the business partner's ideas, input and advice will have value, and the stakeholder will look for business partner leadership within that area. In addition, if the business partner presents their advice with confidence, decisiveness, and reputation for rational thinking, this will support the process of expanding their competences into other subjects and issues that the stakeholder is dealing with. This will also support the development and then extension of their expert power.

Referent power

Referent power in relation to business partners and stakeholders has it roots in positive personal affinity with each other. This positive impact will be enhanced by these attributes:

- the team will be more co-operative with each other;
- they will support each other in adversity;
- increases to the individual's self worth;
- the respect of diversity and opinions;
- individuals will be more open to new ideas rather than resist them.

In the long term, depending on this power base alone can be a poor tactic to be applied. It is necessary to combine these power bases with the specific knowledge, skills and competences that can be applied to productive outcomes that are being sought or targeted.

Information power

Information as a result of holding or owning data that stakeholders and teams require is a source of power. Historically, because of manual and paper-based methods, data and information has not been readily available. In our current digital age, data and information have become increasingly commoditized and readily available. The ability to extract, interpret and analyse is becoming increasingly specialized and this is where the business partner can add insight for the stakeholder. It is the value of the information and its potential use that creates value, and therefore power. This is steadily assuming more importance with the advance of techniques such as 'big data', which is covered in detail within Chapter 6.

In summary, the most effective leaders utilize, in the main, the direct influence of:

- information and its efficient use (information power);
- personality in persuading others (referent power);
- the application of knowledge, skills and competences (expert power).

By using these leadership qualities, the business partner will have a defining impact on their stakeholders, teams and their organization, beyond their current business partner role. If motivated and supported they. in effect, will have the skill set to become potential leaders.

The power of the stakeholder in relation to the business partner

Legitimate power

Legitimate power is the acceptance that a superior has the appropriate accountability:

- to set objectives for the individual;
- to set, monitor, and apply polices and procedures;
- to expect adherence to their requirements.

Legitimate power can rapidly change due to a variety of circumstances that can include changing directives from higher-level executives in the organization, new organizational structures being put in place, a new CEO, and change of responsibilities.

Legitimate power although will apply in the short term it is transitory over the medium to long term The business partner will require to be aware of and adapting to any power changes.

Reward power

This is the power for the right to reward an individual. This may include a mix of quantitative and qualitative elements.

Quantitative elements include decision making and application of:

- salary increases
- size of bonuses
- ex-gratia payments.

Qualitative elements include:

- attractive job enrichment and enlargement
- supporting and advocating career progression
- interesting or high-profile projects.

When business partners anticipate that they will be rewarded for achieving what stakeholders are expecting, there will be a high probability that the outputs or outcomes will be delivered to the objectives, goals and targets that have been established.

The weakness with this power base includes:

- the superior may be in a position of only recommending the rewards and does not have absolute discretion;
- similarly, career progression may be subject to company policies such as equal opportunities and diversity requirements of the organization;
- over-use of rewards could develop that this as an expected norm to be always applied, rather than a true incentive, e.g. bonuses;
- in addition, where rules are not being adhered to, ethics and professional standards may be under tension.

Coercive power

Coercive power is the acceptance that a superior can discipline an individual when objectives are not achieved; policies, or procedures are not adhered too. If not applied with sensitivity, fairly and with integrity, a coercive approach can create problems, including:

- creating a culture of fear;
- increased staff turnover;
- individual and team demotivation;
- poor team cultures.

Summary

In summary, power between a business partner and their stakeholder:

- is relationship based;
- is founded on perceptions;
- is dependent on the different types of power;
- reinforces the enabling or disabling impact upon outcomes;
- enables or constrains the development of good teamwork;
- is a prerogative that can be used wisely or foolishly abused.

To appreciate and understand power relationships will lead to the development of the formation of a productive working relationship based on mutual trust.

Personal and stakeholder team assessments

There are various models to assess and appraise the profile of a business partner and the stakeholder team that they may operate within.

The potential methods that the business partner could apply for personal and stakeholder assessments now follow. The examples are to create awareness of them rather than a detailed explanation of their use and application.

These models support:

- a self- review of the business partner's personal values and beliefs;

- an assessment of the individual profiles within the teams and also the business partners that they operate within.

Personal values and beliefs

A self-review of personal values and beliefs may support the business partner in engaging with and forming productive relationships with stakeholders who may have different value systems and beliefs. Our personal values and beliefs influence the decisions we take, and potentially how we might make choices within our decision-making processes. Our respective family upbringings, social environments and academic influences inextricably impact our values and beliefs.

The self-awareness of the business partner's conscious bias will help support the business partner relationships to minimize any potential conflicts. However, unconscious biases may be inadvertently disclosed to stakeholders and potentially create conflict and strained relationships. The foundation of our personal values is our personal and cultural traits.

Personal traits

These include:
- age
- ethnicity
- sexual orientation
- mental capabilities
- gender.

Cultural traits

These include:
- social status
- nationality
- language
- appearance
- location
- education.

Individual team members may have differing and diverse attributes. The matrix in Figure 2.5 outlines potential approaches to differing personal and cultural traits that the business partner may adopt with stakeholders that have similar or different personal and cultural value traits.

The approaches that can be adopted are:

- When the business partner has acceptable and compatible traits with a stakeholder they could use these to exploit to develop the relationship.
- Where the business partner is faced with incompatible traits from the stakeholder and the business partner traits are acceptable they should seek to maintain and to tolerate.

PERSONAL VALUE MATRIX	BUSINESS PARTNER	
	Incompatible	Acceptable
R	eptable	MAINTAIN TOLERANCE	EXPLOIT DEVELOP
	Incompatible	AVOID CONFLICT	ACKNOWLEDGE RESPECT

es matrix

- When the bus... ess partner may have uncomfortable traits, and are acceptable to the stakeholder they should acknowledge the respect provided.
- Where both the business partner and stakeholder have uncomfortable traits, which are incompatible, then any potential conflicts should be avoided. Personal and cultural differences will have already been deeply established before any business relationships have even commenced. Considered self-awareness, relevant openness and respect are important for the business partner to reflect upon and then move on towards stakeholder team assessments.

Stakeholder team assessments

There are several models that can be applied to team profiles and relationships, and only one example is outlined in this section. These separate role types where initially identified and then developed by Belbin (1989). He ultimately identified eight differing profiles for roles that performed within a team. The insight he provided was that it was the personal preferences of individuals as to their own work style, rather than the formality of job tiles or position within a team. Specific role profiles within a team may identify individuals, capabilities, strengths or weaknesses that are best applied within that team. This may impact how the business partner may react to and behave with other team members, as well as how they examine their own ideal role within that team.

This analysis in relation to business partnering can be utilized to:

- identify strengths and weaknesses within the team;
- raise self-awareness and personal effectiveness;

- build productive working relationships for the business partner;
- support the development of trust and understanding;
- identify any gaps or shortfalls in stakeholder teams;
- create a balance within teams of the various roles.

The various team roles (Wikipedia, n.d.) and their potential positive and negative attributes that have been identified are:

Plant

Potential positive attributes of the role of the plant include:
- imaginative;
- originate new ideas;
- intelligent;
- provide powerful insights.

Potential adverse attributes may include:
- ignore detail and get bored;
- revisiting fundamental points when a course of action has been agreed and accepted by the team;
- can be disruptive.

Resource investigator

Potential positive attributes of the role of the resource investigator include:
- will engage quickly at the beginning of a team project;
- will have an effective and good network within the organization;
- will look outside the team for ideas and input.

Potential negative attributes of the role of the resource investigator include:
- be poor on detail;
- lose momentum towards the end of a project;
- seeking the next new project before the old one is completed.

Coordinator

Potential positive attributes of the role of the coordinator include:
- likely to take a leadership role;
- has a wide perspective on issues;
- good delegation skills;
- recognizing the competences of the team and how they can be best applied.

Potential negative attributes of the role of the coordinator include:
- over-delegating to other team members;
- perceived by other team members as being lazy and not really contributing to the tasks that are required by all the team.

Shaper

Potential positive attributes of the role of the shaper include:
- high energy and keeps the momentum going;
- task and achievement focused;
- provides drive and focus to what is required;
- extroverted and challenging to the rest of the team.

Potential negative attributes of the role of the shaper include:
- perceived as aggressive by other team members;
- over-pushy on other team members;
- impatient;
- intolerant on any delay or perceived failure by other team members.

Monitor evaluator

Potential positive attributes of the role of the monitor evaluator include:
- have an independent perspective;
- logical in their approach;
- good at forwarding options and problem solving on a broad basis.

Potential negative attributes of the role of the evaluator include:
- uninspiring in their approach;
- can be over-critical;
- move slowly.

Team worker

Potential positive attributes of the role of the team worker include:
- good communicators within the team;
- will focus on team harmony and consensus;
- good listeners to other points of view.

Potential negative attributes of the role of the team worker include:
- can be indecisive;
- will avoid conflict.

Implementer

Potential positive attributes of the role of the implementer include:
- grasps the teams members ideas and seeks to implement them;
- good personal discipline upon the tasks and actions allocated to them;
- will be loyal to the team.

Potential negative attributes of the role of the implementer include:

- can be perceived as rigid in their personal tasks at the expense of the team needs;
- will not deviate from the plan or direction that has been established.

Finisher

Potential negative attributes of the role of the finisher include:
- sets high standards for themselves;
- perfectionist;
- accuracy.

Potential negative attributes of the role of the finisher include:
- focusing on unimportant details at the expense of the bigger picture or requirements;
- poor delegators;
- can miss deadlines.

Specialist

Potential negative attributes of the role of the specialist include:
- have excellent skills, knowledge and competences within their area of expertise;
- will positively and proactively share their expertise with the team.

Potential negative attributes of the role of the specialist include:
- activities and tasks outside their expertise they may be indifferent;
- will have a restrictive and limited view and broader issues impacting the team.

The specialist team role was not part of the initial role profiles and was included later by Belbin.

Summary

The inter-personal dynamics of the team are critical for the initiation of effective business partnering. Within the profile types each team member will have a mix of all the attributes, however one or two may dominate, and this will become the role they prefer and are comfortable within a team context.

An assessment of personal and stakeholder team reviews will support the strengthening of the working relationships. This assessment and analysis should ideally be undertaken at the start or early beginning of the business relationship. This assessment will help to support the business partner to what may be the best team position to adopt.

The different styles of business partnering

Successful partnerships will have attributes of tangible benefits, intangible benefits and a mix of both. These will influence the style of business partnering that should be considered.

Tangible benefits:

- stay on track towards their goals;
- the support required for stakeholder outcomes;
- understanding how the team works and how best to support all members.

Intangible benefits:

- the development of trust between all team members;
- engaging with stakeholders and their teams on a amicable basis;
- enhancing the skills and provide a development culture for the team.

A mix of tangible and intangible benefits:

- improve the speed and quality of decision-making;
- cross-team skills enhancement;
- nurture new ideas that will support team goals;
- clear accountabilities and responsibilities for all.

The key output of the above is that differing styles can deliver these outcomes for differing circumstances, requirements, objectives, and outcomes. The internal change requirement or external pressures will help determine which style is more appropriate (Figure 2.6).

Figure 2.6 Style types

The four styles of business partnering (Raymond 2001) that can be applied are:

The regulator

A regulator enforces or imposes the rules for monitoring, observation and compliance that are required. The features of this style will include:

- rule and compliance based;
- reactive by nature;
- status quo is sought or upheld;
- implements the requirements of organizations strategy;
- operationally focused;
- dealing with operational defects;
- knowledge will include the detailed processes that need to be adhered to;
- skills will include the immediate rectification of defects and, when required, more serious defects are brought to their immediate superior;
- competences will include maintaining the application of the detailed rules and regulations, and a comprehensive understanding why and how they apply.

The service provider

Service providers will provide support on the basis of specific needs that have been identified and agreed.
   The features of this style will include the following features:

- creating a flexible environment;
- incremental change;
- change management will be supply led;
- facilitates the operational process implementation;
- operational efficiency focus;
- solution providing;
- skills will include details of systems and processes;
- knowledge of the end-to-end business processes;
- competences will include a proficient understanding for customer advice.

The change agent

A change agent assertively promotes the culture change or organizational transformation that is being sought. The features of this style will include:

- commitment to the organization's culture;
- interventionist by nature;
- the ability to implement and manage the change;
- will be part of the strategic choices being considered;

- project-based management;
- developing option and solution choices;
- skills will include the management of complex interrelated projects;
- knowledge of strengths, weaknesses and the opportunities of the change.

The business partner will have to deploy different business partner styles in various circumstances. These will be influenced by result of a variety of reasons. These include the following:

- acquisition of new businesses, either locally, nationally or globally;
- different systems and processes in local business units;
- customer delivery variations;
- historical reasons e.g. the structure of decentralized business with local power bases;
- merger with another business;
- stakeholders resisting change;
- trade union resistance.

In addition there may be different styles of business partnering within the organization and these will have different advantages and disadvantages.

The business advisor

The business advisor will proactively engage with stakeholders with their skills, knowledge, and competences.

The features of this style will include:

- being flexible on the requirements being requested;
- proactive by nature;
- change will be demand led;
- provides intelligence based upon strategy;
- has an effectiveness focus;
- problem-solving attributes;
- skills will include high levels of technical proficiency;
- detailed knowledge based on expertise;
- competences which will include professional and insightful advice provision.

Advantages for different styles of business partnering within an organization

From a business partnering perspective there are a few advantages of having multiple ways of working. However, there may be some organizational advantages for doing this, and these are:

- when the cost of standardization may be high;

- when the cost of implementing standard systems may be too high;
- where stakeholders prefer different ways of working then there will be less resistance from them;
- there may be some legacy processes, which will disappear over time;
- there may be some legal reasons for different ways in different countries;
- there may be insufficient staff resources to manage the change;
- there may be some processes where the volumes are so low that it is more cost effective to have more than one way of working.

Disadvantages for different styles of business partnering within an organization

From a business partner's perspective, there are several issues that arise from having several methods of working. These are:

- added costs for running multiple systems and processes;
- compliance is more difficult to manage;
- cycle times of processing are potentially increased;
- increased levels or potential defects may occur;
- difficulty in standardizing processes may result;
- barriers for implementing new systems and technologies;
- increased complexity of service level agreements (SLAs) or contractual agreements;
- management of activities is more complex and challenging;
- training staff on multiple practices and systems becomes more of a challenge;
- restricted opportunity occurs to build to scale;
- different controls environments are needed;
- more difficulty in benchmarking performance, e.g. comparing inconsistent data or information sets;
- restriction of business continuity options.

The merging of styles

A further degree of complexity is that the four styles may, in practice, be combined versions of two or more styles. These will be influenced by the following operating requirements from stakeholders:

- the level of engagement of stakeholders for the co-design of the governance and regular reviews of outcomes being achieved;
- the level of engagement with stakeholders to support the management of risks and the level of trust to improve decision making;
- the degree of definition of timings and outcomes that is required;
- the degree and level of acceptance and integration by the stakeholder;
- the clarity of identity and commitment from stakeholders for their needs;
- the process and style of evaluating and communicating performance.

In summary, for the business partner to be effective they will need to have an awareness of what style is anticipated by the relevant stakeholder and what their expectations are. This assessment will be influenced or determined by the degree of flexibility that the business partner is permitted or will be accepted by their stakeholders. In addition the stakeholder operating requirements will also influence the style(s) to be adopted by the business partner. Once the optimum style has been assimilated, the key issue for the stakeholder will be the team priorities and how the business partner may positively impact upon them.

PREPARING FOR THE ENGAGEMENT WITH THE ORGANIZATION

The appraisal of the organizational culture, using situational analysis and deciding the immediate priorities will support the business partner's engagement with the organization.

Appraising the culture of the organization

To prepare for how the business partner will support the team's engagement with the organization, the organizational culture should be assessed. Yet the definition of culture is a difficult concept to describe. A list of 164 differing definitions where compiled by Kroeber and Kluckhohn in 1952. Apte (1994: 2001) in contributing to a 10-volume encyclopaedia of language and linguistics, noted that even after over one hundred years there was still no consensus upon an agreed definition of culture. Avruch (1998: 14) also forwards the proposition that 'there are mutually related ideas about culture that are considered still inadequate'.

Cultural features can be applied and be considered within a business partnering relationship:

- The culture of an organization is uniform across it in relation to behaviours, in that they provide a norm that will be accepted.
- How to act and behave will be learned quickly by the reinforcement of peer and team pressure.
- Variations to the general excepted norms may be perceived as aberrant to the organization's expectations.
- A new member of the team will be expected to conform the traditions and customs that are already have been established.

Potential key issues that the new business partner needs to consider are:

1   They need to be conscious of the culture of the organization.
2   They are unlikely to change the culture as an individual.
3   A clear and consistent definition of the organization's culture may not be in place or articulated with any clarity.

More importantly, the business partner needs to develop methods to make an impact on the culture. A new idea will be likely to be accepted within the organizational norms if these conditions are met:

1 It is consistent with existing cultural patterns, it does not confront them.
2 It is accepted to be superior to what already exists.
3 Those who are affected easily understand it.
4 It is able to be tested and challenged by stakeholders.
5 The benefits and opportunities are clearly visible to the relevant stakeholders.
6 The risks and threats are known and have been mitigated for the stakeholder.
7 The change or innovation is understood and accepted.

When the business partner has an appreciation of how and why the cultural norms are taken into consideration and adopted within the organization, the more tangible the assessments will have a context to relate to. Situational appraisal of the organization will focus on what and where the current organizational priorities and aims are.

The initial organizational situational appraisal

The induction process, in the main, relates to the acquisition of detailed knowledge within the partnering role. If the business partner is to fulfil their potential for creating added value within their team, strategic knowledge needs to be identified, reviewed, and assimilated. This strategic appraisal process will empower the business partner to support the team's engagement with the organizational aims and goals. Without this clear alignment, there is a risk of not delivering the support required.

There are several methods that could support the business partner in preparing their team for alignment with strategic and tactical organizational aims. Two example of these are the:

- *The PESTEL model:* this is related to the strategic engagement of the organization in relation to macro business factors.
- *The 5C model:* this is the tactical engagement of the organization within the markets in which it operates.

PESTEL Model

Each organization will have different political, economic, social, technological, environmental and legal drivers, (PESTEL) which will impact on the decisions it makes in relation to business partnering. Some significant drivers impacting business partnering within their organization's PESTEL model are outlined below:

1   Political
   - changing political and regulatory impacts;
   - ethical purchasing and brand awareness and loyalty;
   - the changing dynamics between developed and developing countries.
2   Economic
   - identifying opportunities of growth either organically, through joint ventures or by acquisition;
   - the fluctuation price on the price of oil and its impact upon the global economy;
   - the austerity policies of governments;
   - quantitative easing and its impact on interest and foreign exchange rates.
3   Social
   - the impact of social media;
   - the growth and development of diversity;
   - supply-side factors, such as the number of graduates in the available workforce and the employability of offshore talent.
4   Technological
   - disruptive innovation taking place in business sectors;
   - the increasing level of self-service of information technologies;
   - the rise and potential exponential increase of cloud computing;
   - big data explosion and analytics;
   - an acceleration of the implementation and use of data analytics to drive both purchase and service delivery decisions.
5   Environmental
   - corporate responses to the challenge of reducing the carbon footprint of the organization;
   - the green movement and its impact on the economy;
   - increased focus on sustainability in organizations.
6   Legal
   - intellectual capital and data protection;
   - home country and foreign sector regulation in the UK financial services sector, for example, any institution regulated by financial services legislation has to consider the political and cultural environment in any offshore locations, as well as, the applicability of home data protection legislation and financial regulations, in addition there is increasing EU regulation;
   - offshore country regulation, legal and judicial processes;
   - cross-border controls on the movement of personal data.

The above PESTEL trends were topical at the time of writing, however the degree of adjustment to any PESTEL analysis is intensifying due to increasing volatility, uncertainty, change and ambiguity (VUCA) of the world that organizations operate in. Business partners, if they are to add value and avoid risk to the stakeholders they support, have a requirement to keep abreast of changes that impact their organizations.

The 5C model

5C analysis of the company, competitors, customers, collaborators and business climate is a method of exploring the framework that an organization operates in, and will provide additional insights how a business partner can act upon.

Company

The review of an organization should include its mission and vision statement and its goals. This review will provide the business partner the reliability of the organization's operating model. This analysis will provide insights of strengths, weaknesses, opportunities and threats.

Competitors

The analysis of competitors will highlight the relativities and differences within the market place. This will help the business partner to identify critical success factors for the organization to focus upon. This will then allow the development of capabilities that can be exploited against other organizations operating in the same markets.

Customers

The examination of key customers can be complex and may relate to both internal and external customers. This may include customer needs, the motivation to purchase the product, sales levels, purchasing power, frequency and value of sales, market size, and growth opportunities.

Collaborators

These relationships are also business-partnering collaborators. These are important for businesses as they provide support for the development of additional new ideas and opportunities, for example suppliers, distributors of the product and joint ventures.

Climate

The context of climate is the business environment that the organization operates in. The PESTEL model is a useful method to undertake this examination, review and then develop insights that lead to actions.

Summary

In conclusion, the direct organizational impact of the business partner engagement may be limited. However analysing, gaining knowledge, and increasing skill levels, by using relevant methods, will have the direct benefits of:

- increasing the business partner's competences towards leadership roles;
- supporting the alignment of the individual with team goals;
- providing a context when organizational challenges impact the team;
- developing an agile approach to change.

Impact and priority matrix

In approaching the end of this chapter we have reviewed the preparation of engagement by the individual business partner, by team(s) and the potential engagement with the organizational goals. It is unlikely that the depth of understanding and knowledge absorbed within an initial induction program will be sufficient to prepare the business partner fully to make the business impact required. In addition, a full team and strategic analysis of the organization might not be relevant or useful to the business partner. The practical agile checklist in Table 2.3 has been developed and utilized by the author on numerous occasions both as a consultant, within business partnering roles and in mentoring and coaching business partners.

The impact assessment for the business partner is shown in Table 2.3. Once the initial impact assessment is made, the issues can be mapped upon an impact/priority impact matrix (Table 2.4). This will help to determine the priorities that the business partner should focus upon and in what order. Increasing and critical issues will take priority over less urgent and stable issues. Stable or decreasing issues can be placed on hold. The issues identified and analysed will support the targeting and priority of stakeholder engagement (Table 2.4).

Upon assessment and completion of the impact/priority matrix, the potential initial targets for attention for the business partner can be determined.

In summary, the degree and depth of individual, team and organizational preparation and engagement by the business partner will help to support:

- The transition to the acceptance stage of the business-partnering model.
- A quicker transit through the acceptance stage towards delivery.

Table 2.3 The initial framework

What are the legacy issues that need to be addressed?
- Has there been a handover which has been fully documented within a disposition statement?
- Has there been a verbal handover?
- No business handover has taken place.

What technologies are available and the medium-term time to access them?
- What is the scope of technology, data, information and analytics availability:
  - Functional?
  - Enterprise?
  - Big data?
- Is the IT department a true enabler for information use or is it a constraint?

What are the key deliverables that need to take place?
- Are they financial?
- Are they non-financial?
- Are they short, medium or long term?

Who are the key internal stakeholders?
- The initial induction may not introduce all the key stakeholders that the business partner needs to interact with. Have these been identified and contacted?

Who do the internal stakeholders need to influence and interact with?
- Is it internal stakeholders?
- Is it external stakeholders?
- Is it a few senior executives?
- Is it a wide community of stakeholders across the business?

What are the initial constraints?
- Is it your stakeholders time?
- Is it financial restraints?
- It it time constraints e.g. a project running late.

What are the key products and services to be supported and in what priority?
- Is there a new product launch?
- Any issues with existing products and markets?

What is the core business model?
- Is it static, how long has it been the same?
- Has it changed?
- Are there new board members with different expectations?

Table 2.4 Impact/priority matrix

	Hold	Urgent	Critical
Increasing			
Stable			
Decreasing			

Chapter summary

To prepare is to make (something) ready for use or consideration. There are several governance models that can be considered and this will influence the initial induction process. A strategic review will impact which priorities are required; this will be supported by relevant knowledge, skills and competences of the business partner. An assessment of personal values, beliefs, ethics, culture, personal, and trust will improve the support to stakeholders. Models and different styles of business partnering will support the positive engagement and initial impact with stakeholders. The requirement for the personal responsibility for self-learning and induction was outlined and is fundamental to the effectiveness of a business partner. The power style of the stakeholder impacts their teams and also the business partner. This will then influence the style that should be adopted by the business partner. Reviewing the organization's culture and situation it is currently placed in will determine the impacts and priorities that the business partner should prepare and then focus upon.

We now move to the Stage 2 of the general model, which is engagement. To engage is to consent to receive or undertake something which is offered.

References

Acevedo, J.M. & Yancey, G.B. (2011) 'Assessing new employee orientation programs', *Journal of Workplace Learning*, 23(5): 349–354.

Apte, M. (1994) 'Language in sociocultural context'. In: R. E. Asher (ed.), *The Encyclopaedia of Language and Linguistics*. Vol.4 (pp. 2000–2010). Oxford: Pergamon Press.

Avruch, K. (1998) *Culture and Conflict Resolution*. Washington DC: United States Institute of Peace Press.

Belbin, M. (1981). *Management Teams*. London: Heinemann.

Kroeber, A. L. and Kluckhohn, C. (1952) *Culture: A Critical Review of Concepts and Definitions*. Cambridge, MA: The Museum.

Raven, B. H. (1965). 'Social influence and power'. In I.D. Steiner and M. Fishbein (Eds.), *Current Studies in Social Psychology* (pp. 371–382). New York: Holt, Rinehart, Winston.

Raymond, C. (2001) 'Champions, adapters, consultants, and synergists: the new change agents in HRM'. *Human Resource Management Journal,* 11(3): 39–52.

Wikipedia (n.d.) 'Team role inventories'. Retrieved 8 March 2015 from http://en.wikipedia.org/wiki/Team_Role_Inventories.

3   The engagement stage

Engage: To occupy or attract someone's interest or attention.

(Oxford Dictionaries Online)

The only way to do great work is to love what you do.

(Steve Jobs)

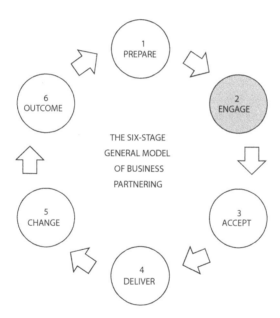

Figure 3.1 Engagement overview

This chapter explains the establishment of the engagement process, service content and emotional contract with stakeholders.

Knowledge components considered within this chapter

The engagement expectation

- setting expectations for models that can be applied
- engagement models
- setting expectations.

The psychological contract

- the softer skills and expectations of stakeholders
- partnering from within and outside the function
- profiles and features that impact business partnering.

The service content engagement

- power in relation to engagement
- the alignment of team and corporate goals
- the business partnering relationships within matrix frameworks.

THE SETTING OF EXPECTATIONS

If the business partner's aims are to create enterprise value and excel in their role, there is a requirement to understand the complexity of stakeholder engagement. Different models that might be adopted and applied may influence the style of engagement. Effective engagement should also consider the impact on softer issues that will build and support effective relationships. Working in a matrix relationship of some form is probable for the business partner. Therefore, understanding the legitimacy, urgency and power of a stakeholder and how this impacts the relationship will become a critical component of effective engagement.

Setting expectations for models that can be applied

Setting expectations is a critical requirement that needs to be positioned between the business partner and their key stakeholders. To seek agreement of 'who does what' requires mutual understanding, dependency and acceptance by all relevant parties.

Expectations relate to the effort that will result in the attainment of the required outputs or outcomes. The business partner's and stakeholder's skills, knowledge, and competences should support collaborative methods for the convergence of the required team goals. There are four features that will support the convergence of team or joint outcomes. These are:

1 *Perceived goal attainment:* Goals should ideally provide a stretch and also be attainable. When they are set to unreasonably high standards an individual

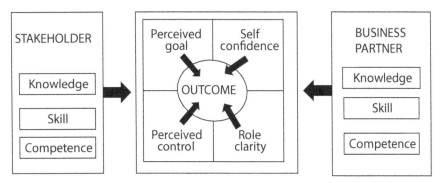

Figure 3.2 Outcomes

or team will have the belief that their desired targets are unattainable. Setting achievable goals will increase engagement and motivation.

2 *Self-confidence:* This is based upon the individual's perspective about their skills to achieve the goals required. They will self-evaluate if they have the requisite knowledge and competences that can be applied to meet the expectations required.

3 *Perceived control:* Individuals within a team must trust each other to contribute collectively. If the team perceives that the expectations of them are an unreasonable stretch and, in effect, they are not in control, this will result in low expectations of effective delivery of the team goals. It is important that the team feels psychologically in control.

4 *Role clarity:* The purpose of a role clarification is to provide all team members clear expectation of their responsibilities, accountabilities and interdependencies upon each other. This will increase team efficiency and effectiveness.

Interdependent team projects, or in situations where people have unclear responsibilities, creating a framework for common expectations becomes critically important. Without agreement, common understanding and clarity, it is likely that gaps, duplication, and confusion will occur. Teamwork will become frustrated, inefficient and less likely to deliver the identified and desired goals. The use or choice of which engagement model to adopt will help support:

- the balance of perceived goals;
- the assessment of the perceived control requirement;
- the mutual confidence for both parties;
- the required role clarity to deliver the outcomes required.

These are attributes of good team performance and the opposite will apply to poorly performing teams.

Engagement models

The engagement and development of the relationship between the business partner and the stakeholder will vary within a range of both formal and informal arrangements. In Chapter 2, we outlined the dimensions of individual, team, and organizational preparedness. These will then impact upon the level of formality of the relationship. This includes the assessment, use, and application of:

- governance models that are in use
- business drivers for the relationship
- orientation of the relationship
- level of trust
- culture of the organization
- ethics boundaries.

Within the range of contractual formality and consensual informality, four types of models can be defined and applied:

- the contractual model
- the service level agreement model
- the objective-setting model
- the laissez-faire model.

In support of and alignment to these models, four emerging styles that can be applied to business partnering were reviewed in Chapter 2: the regulator, the business advisor, the service provider and the change agent. These can now be broadly aligned to the types of models that are impacted.

The features of the model types and how the dimensions of business partnering impact them are illustrated and explained in Figure 3.3.

The contractual model

A contract is a methodical, documented, legally binding formal agreement between a business partner and the primary stakeholder. This type of model will normally apply to outsourced relationships.

Different jurisdictions will have different features. An initial example under English law that provides proof of a contractual relationship will include:

- an offer
- acceptance of the offer
- valid consideration.

A second example under USA law, forming a contract would include the obligations of:

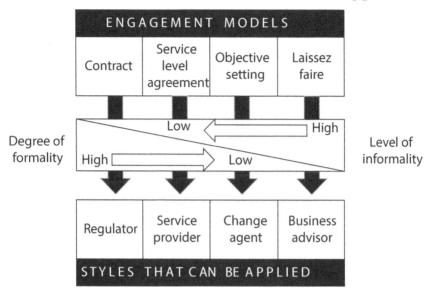

Figure 3.3 Engagement models

- agreement
- consideration and estoppel
- formality
- privity.

Both the business partner and primary stakeholder will have rights on and duties to each other, and in addition both parties will expect an acceptable benefit from the contract.

Selected business partnering arrangements can be outsourced and contractual conditions are more likely to be applied to those cases. For example IT (information technology) and HR (human resources) functions are two typical business functions that may have outsourced activities and responsibilities for business partnering. The impact elements and key features are outlined in Table 3.1

The regulator style will be the most suitable alignment to the contractual model. In some instances the contractual model may also include or refer to service level agreements.

Service level agreements (SLA)

Service level agreements can be both referenced within a contract or a model in their own right. Service level agreements are used to define the level of service that will exist between the provider (the business partner) and their 'customers' (stakeholders) that might be either internal or external. The language will be

Table 3.1 Contractual model

The impact of	Features
Governance models that are applied	A formal contract will be in place that will include clearly stated offer to provide a service for financial consideration
Business drivers for the relationship	The principal feature will be financial consideration for delivery of required outputs: • The initial induction process should include an understanding of the key requirements of the contract. • Situational appraisal at a macro level will deem the outsourcing risk as low. • Any added value impacts are likely to be defined within the contract, and any variations will be subject to contract amendment. Professional competences, knowledge, skills and competences will be outside the organization
Orientation of the relationship	May be potentially adversarial by nature of the contract requirements upon delivery requirements. In addition the contract clauses may include a service level agreement clauses to measure the effectiveness of the contract.
Level of trust	Boundaries of trust are clearly defined
Culture of the organization	'Hands off' from the detail delivery Outsourcing and contractual perspective on relationships
Ethics boundaries	Based on the legal jurisdiction of the agreed contract

much simpler than a legal contract so that both parties understand it without legal support or advice. The SLA should include the availability of the service, performance levels, how it will operate, priorities and responsibilities. There are likely to be agreed targets and a measurement system being positioned as the primary focus of the working relationship.

Service level agreement models will normally apply to inter-functional and intra organizational relationships, for example, HR to finance within the same organization. This will be influenced by where the reporting lines for the business partner and stakeholder to senior executives are aligned too.

The impact elements and key features are outlined in Table 3.2.

The objective-setting model

Clear objectives will establish what the business partner and stakeholders are planning or targeting to achieve. It is critical for both parties that the process of setting objectives is robust. Specific and measurable objectives provide a framework for the working relationship. Attainable and sensible targets will increase motivation levels of individuals, and also the team. These will specify what outputs or outcomes are to be delivered.

Table 3.2 Service level agreement model

The impact of	Features
Governance models that are applied	Both parties will approve a service level agreement. This will be based on the elements of some or all of the profile above.
Business drivers for the relationship	The drivers are: • The initial induction process will be based on the requirements of the service level contract. • Situational appraisal at a micro level will deem the relationship risk as very low or outsourcing to be of little value. • Any added value impacts are likely to be reviewed on a regular (at least annual) basis and normally subject to variations to the SLA. • Professional competences, knowledge, skills, and competences will be inside the organization.
Orientation of the relationship	Will focus on agreed parameters to be performance measured, e.g. both key performance indicators and detailed operating indicators. These will be reviewed and discussed by both parties on regular and agreed intervals. An expectation to improve these indicators.
Level of trust	The service level agreement will be signed by both parties, however the clauses and requirements should be fewer, less complex and demanding than a formal contract.
Culture of the organization	Collaborative in nature and to provide the service required.
Ethics boundaries	The ethics of the organization will apply.

Peter Drucker (1955) and G.T. Doran are generally accredited for developing the SMART concept. The SMART concept is based on five attributes that effective targets should include. These are:

• **S**pecific
• **M**easurable
• **A**chievable
• **R**ealistic
• **T**ime bound.

This method of target setting is now used in many organizations. The business partnering relationship, adopting the objective-setting model, may be driven by:

• the function that the business partner belongs to;
• the stakeholder that the business partner engages with;
• a combination of both.

Table 3.3 Objective-setting model

The impact of	Features
Governance models that are applied	Both parties will approve a service level agreement. This will be based on the elements of some or all of the profile above.
Business drivers for the relationship	The drivers are: • The initial induction process will be based on the requirements of the service level contract. • Situational appraisal at a micro level will deem the relationship risk as very low or outsourcing to be of little value. • Any added value impacts are likely to be reviewed on a regular (at least annual) basis and normally subject to variations to the SLA. • Professional competences, knowledge, skills, and competences will be inside the organization.
Orientation of the relationship	Will focus on agreed parameters to be performance measured. e.g. both key performance indicators and detailed operating indicators. These will be reviewed and discussed by both parties on regular and agreed intervals. An expectation to improve these indicators.
Level of trust	The service level agreement will be signed by both parties, however the clauses and requirements should be fewer, less complex and demanding than a formal contract.
Culture of the organization	Collaborative in nature and to provide the service required.
Ethics boundaries	The ethics of the organization will apply.

As described above, the business partner will be part of the agreement process and acceptance of the objectives. The impact elements and key features are outlined Table 3.3.

Laissez-faire model

The French phrase *laissez faire* literally means, 'let them do.' It was first used in 1751 to describe how the French state should promote commerce. However, over time the current usage relates to 'let it be,' or 'leave it alone.' Business partnering towards a laissez-faire model can be relevant where the business partnering relationship is of an advisory, or infrequent usage basis. An example of this may be the relationship with a communications department for the organization (Table 3.4)

The business advisor style will be the most suitable alignment for this model.

In summary, the degree of formal and informal arrangements that the business partner may need to negotiate with a stakeholder will have dependencies that are unique to each function or organization. Once the arrangements have been established, engagement expectations need to be understood and acknowledged.

Table 3.4 Laissez-faire model

Impact of	Features
Governance models that are applied	No formal detail frameworks are likely to be in place, however both the stakeholder and business partner will be aware of the broad service requirements.
Business drivers for the relationship	On a demand and request basis. Tend to be unique requirements by nature of the business partners professional; knowledge, skills, and competences, and will be of high value and significance.
Orientation of the relationship	Non-interventionist, dealing with requests when they occur.
Level of trust	Very high levels of trust, partly based on reliance of professional competence.
Culture of the organization	The advisory model will apply to support the requirements.
Ethics boundaries	The individual performing the service will integrate with their professional ethics and standards.

The expectations need to be set regardless of the style of business partnering alignment and the model of formality that may be applied.

Setting expectations

Conflicting expectations are a common feature for any organization. A range of internal, external and personal factors or attributes will determine the degree of the potential level of conflict and its resulting impact. The internal factors will include: time-related deadlines, cash constraints, and service dependencies from third parties, and potential different perspectives of compliance and ethics. External factors may also have been initially identified through the impact/priority matrix (see Chapter 2). The skills, knowledge, and competences of the business partner and stakeholder will also influence the identification of any potential conflicts.

The initial identification of conflict requires an open-minded perspective on the potential range of possibilities rather than fixing upon one single point of view. Conflicting goals are within a range and the potential conflict will vary in its range and complexity as illustrated in Figure 3.4.

One of the key features at the first stage of the business partner and stakeholder relationship will be the initial identification of acceptance or resistance to goals, targets, or objectives. Initial discussions may move resistance to a hostile push-back from the stakeholder, or alternatively towards a positive acceptance and then full agreement. The models defined previously will directly impact upon the identification of goals and how they might be resolved. An examination of how the bias of the models of contract, services level agreement, objective-setting and laissez-faire models impact engagement or conflict now follows.

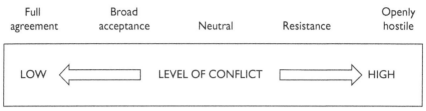

Figure 3.4 Range of conflicts

The contractual model

The features include:

- The contractual model identification of conflict will be highlighted through the negotiation process. e.g. price, service levels, delivery times.
- Any potential engagement issues are likely to be identified at the start of the negotiations.
- Processes of dealing with conflict and engagement processes are likely to be included within the risks and rewards embedded within the contract.

The service model

The features include:

- The measures and key performance indicators (KPIs) that are to be included within the service level agreement will identify the potential conflicts e.g. the service definition is unclear or has not been fully understood.
- Positive engagement will also be used on activities or expectations that have not been specifically included within the initial SLA.
- The processes of resolving any engagement conflicts could be based on using the RACI model, review of KPIs and the review meetings that will take place on service levels.

The objective-setting model

The features include:

- The establishment and initial agreement of the objective setting will identify any potential conflicts.
- The process of clarifying engagement is likely to be based upon, utilizing the SMART model, appraisals, and 'one to one' review meetings.
- The relative power level of the stakeholder in relation to the business partner will define the resolution of engagement issues.

The laissez-faire model

The features include:

- At the initial stages it is unlikely that conflict might occur, by definition laissez-faire is to leave alone.
- The demand for the usage of service may create capacity constraints for the provider and this will identify potential conflicts to the timing of providing the service.
- The supply or interjection of the provider through either compliance or ethical issues may create a source of potential conflict identification.

Any potential conflicts by the business partner at the initial engagement stage will support the mitigation of risk with stakeholder relationship. On identification of any potential conflict there are several techniques that the business partner should deploy or consider:

- request more thinking time;
- examine the facts;
- review the emotional levels of the potential conflict;
- seek clarification from the stakeholder;
- review what the root cause of the conflict might be;
- review if the conflict has an input, process issue, or is output based;
- the power of the stakeholder, which is critical, and this is examined below.

Resolving and dealing with conflict is covered in more detail in Chapter 4.

THE PSYCHOLOGICAL CONTRACT

The softer skills and expectations of stakeholders

In a business partner/stakeholder relationship the psychological contract is the perspective that two or more parties will have in relation to their joint emotional support for each other. This will include compassion, empathy, fairness, respect and trust for each other. When the softer skills and ethical values are in place, mutual aims and goals can be potentially accelerated, as there is less conflict resolution to take place within the relationship and more time can be focused on achieving the targets required.

Expectations

The softer skills that are required for the business partner are effectively embodied in the social skills within a psychological contract. A psychological contract can be defined as the perceptions of two parties of what their mutual requirements and expectations are towards each other. These requirements will often be informal and imprecise. These will be influenced by:

- what has happened in the past;
- current experiences;
- expectations for the future.

There are three levels that may impact upon the personal obligations and expectations between a business partner and the stakeholders they support.

First, at a macro level, the culture of where the relationships are based will have an impact upon the contract, e.g. different country cultures and values vary and need to be respected.

Second, the psychological contract will be partly influenced at an organizational level through corporate values, often defined and articulated within their mission and vision statements.

Third, individual social interactions at a micro or individual level will influence the behavioural norms and will have a strong impact upon the psychological contract.

The ethical impact upon softer skills

The ethics and social interaction of the business partner with stakeholders at a micro level will be specific, unique and, in the first instance, will be based on their own personal, cultural traits and experiences. Research is still being developed within this area. however Thompson and Hart (2006) outlined thirteen propositions in relation to emotional interaction with ethics and how individuals support the ethics of the organization, the impact on the moral tone of the organization, behaviours and the avoidance of risks relating to moral values. These have been placed into the following groupings of personal, between individuals, and the organization as a whole, and are outlined below:

Personal ethics

1   The number and extent of perceived violations of psychological contracts among employees will be positively correlated with the incidence of employee deviance behaviours in the organization at large.
2   Employees will assign greater moral importance to perceived obligations that the organization is not fulfilling than to those that the organization is fulfilling.
3   Perceived violation of ideological obligations in the psychological contract are more likely to result in feelings of moral outrage than are perceived violations of economic or socio-emotional obligations.

(Thompson and Hart, 2006)

Between individuals of an organization

1   The number and extent of perceived violations of psychological contracts among employees will be positively correlated with incidences of ethical misconduct by the organization at large.

2   Social network position will predict perceptions of psychological contract content and fulfilment/violation.

3   Social network position will predict violation-related deviant behaviours.

4   Management responses to perceived violation, that avoid morally charged language, will result in more dialogue and compromise, than will management responses that appeal to moral imperatives.

(Thompson and Hart, 2006)

The organization as an entity

1   The number and extent of perceived violations of psychological contracts among employees will be positively correlated with the incidence of labour disputes and level of employer/ employee strife in the organization at large.

2   Employees will use more morally charged language when describing obligations that the organization is not fulfilling, than when describing those that the organization is fulfilling.

3   Perceived violation of ideological obligations in the psychological contract are more likely to result in use of morally charged language and invocation of third-party interests by employees in describing the violation than are perceived violations of economic or socio-emotional obligations.

4   Perceived violation of ideological obligations in the psychological contract is more likely to result in principled organizational dissent and whistle blowing, than are perceived violations of economic or socio-emotional obligations.

5   Organizations in which management and employees engage in explicit dialogue about reciprocal obligations upon employee entry, will encounter fewer perceived violations of the psychological contract than will organizations that do not engage in such dialogue.

6   Organizations in which management and employees engage in explicit dialogue about reciprocal obligations upon employee entry, will experience greater openness to discuss perceived obligations (i.e. less moral outrage on the part of employees) in the future.

(Thompson and Hart, 2006)

Personal, cultural, and professional ethics are the key to developing personal and productive relationships. The softer skills and ethics within a productive psychological contract are the perceptions of two parties, of what the mutual requirements and expectations are anticipated towards each other. These requirements will often be informal and imprecise. Without this self-awareness and understanding of these dimensions, the impact of the business partner relationship and outcomes may be diminished. Personal contracts are an integral element of the ongoing relationships between business partners and stakeholders. The psychological contract is influenced at different levels and is based on perceptions, obligations and expectations of both parties. These individual interpretations of psychological expectations may have a weak correlation to the formal obligations of the organization. In summary, the softer psychological loyalties may override organizational aims. The power of this relationship is referent power and needs to be kept in balance with organizational needs.

Partnering from within and outside the function

The importance and relevance of the psychological contract between two parties will vary, and this may impact how the business partner engages with internal and external stakeholders and where they might be best placed. The constantly changing dynamics of the business environment will also make an impact where the business partner might be best placed to support enterprise value.

Internal and external stakeholders

The internal and external relationships that the business partners may have direct or indirect working relationships with are illustrated in Figure 3.5.

Internal stakeholders are likely to include the owners/shareholders, employees and the internal functions they serve. External stakeholders could include society, government, investors, banks, suppliers and customers. The business partner is likely to have one primary stakeholder, which is probably one on the following:

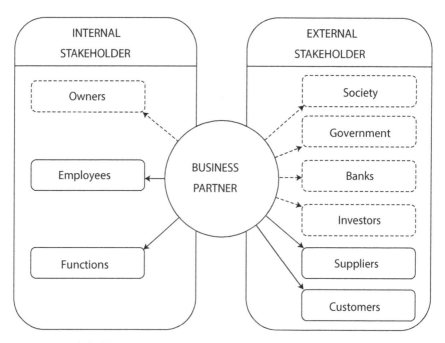

Figure 3.5 Stakeholders

- own function or other functions
- employees
- customers
- suppliers.

Less likely stakeholder groups that the business partner will directly engage with will include society, government, investors or banks. The relationship with these groups will probably be indirect through an intermediary specialist. The PESTEL model will influence whether there is a direct business partner relationship to be established.

The four primary placement models for a business partner

The four placement models of the business partner are:

1 *The functional model:* This will be defined where the business partner is placed within their primary functional specialism and is still within the organization. The focus will be a direct impact upon the outcomes of the stakeholder, e.g. a finance business partner who has direct reporting responsibilities to the finance function and will also include those outside the function, such as general managers, divisional managing directors.
2 *The outsourced model:* This will be defined as a business partner within their primary specialism who aligns directly with the functional requirements that they support, e.g. an outside HR business partner serving HR. The focus will be direct impact upon the outputs, however this is outsourced.
3 *The organizational model:* This will be defined as the business partners who are outside their primary functional specialism but still within the

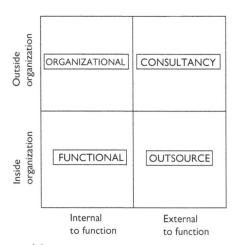

Figure 3.6 Placement model

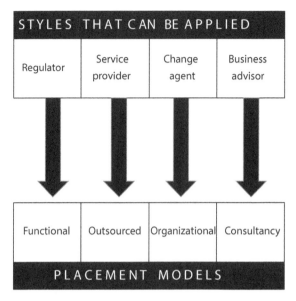

Figure 3.7 Engagement models

organization. The focus for the business partners will be to influence the outcomes of their stakeholders. Their focus will be indirect influence upon the outcomes for the stakeholder, e.g. HR business partner based within the procurement function.

4   *The consultancy model:* The fourth option is in effect a consultancy model where the business partner is outside their primary specialism and is also outside the organization. The focus will be indirect impact upon the outputs and in effect is a consultancy relationship.

The optimum position where the business partner is placed is dependent upon several factors and these include:

- the type of stakeholders that are to be supported, e.g. internal or external stakeholders;
- the PESTEL analysis;
- the VUCA (volatility, uncertainty, complexity, and ambiguity) model;
- the style of the business partnering relationship – the linkages are illustrated in Figure 3.7.

The changing business environment

The VUCA model (Stiehm and Townsend, 2002) model describes the changing business environment that the business partner and stakeholders continually are being challenged with.

Stakeholder and organizational challenges are:

- *Volatile*: Change is a constant and the speed of this continues to accelerate. This can displace the organizations' existing business models with almost immediate impact.
- *Uncertain* There is increasing unpredictability in the markets that organizations operate within and these markets are also becoming increasingly unclear. e.g. Technology convergence.
- *Complex:* The dynamic forces within the PESTEL model identify the increasing complexity of the pressures upon organizations.
- *Ambiguous:* Obscurity and differing perceived realities would create new challenges and an increased incidence of misunderstandings.

The capability of business partners, stakeholders and businesses to utilize the model will include the following elements:

- proactive planning for various scenarios;
- disaster planning and full testing of the plans;
- the integration of functional priorities to the corporate plan;
- training and formal procedures being in place;
- effective financial control and cash management.

The capability of using this method is dependent on the organizational risk profile, the organization's forward planning capabilities, and the base assumptions that are to be deployed. This is where the business partner can create stakeholder and enterprise added value. This will be additionally supported by the optimum placement of the business partner.

Profiles and features that impact business partnering

The position of the business partner may be placed within the organization or outside it. There are several profiles and features that should influence this.

Profiles of stakeholders that business partners may support

To define the potential profiles of stakeholders there are three drivers – power, legitimacy and urgency that will impact an understanding of the type of stakeholder.

The interactions of power, legitimacy, and urgency have linkages with the power/matrix model in relation to the potential interactions that might take place with stakeholders. The following profiles can apply to a stakeholder's position, specific circumstances, or the context of their requirements, rather than being fixed personal traits of the individual.

The interactions of these support the definition of seven stakeholder profiles that are illustrated in Figure 3.8 (Mitchell *et al.*, 1997)

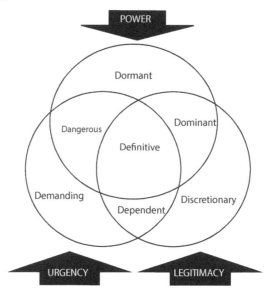

Figure 3.8 Power, legitimacy and urgency

Dormant Stakeholders

These stakeholders will have no or very small engagement within the organization. Although they may not have any legitimacy or creating an immediate sense of urgency, they have the right and capability to apply their power. Dormant stakeholders have the capability to enforce their requirements upon an organization. Examples of dormant stakeholders may include society, government, and regulators.

Dominant stakeholders

Where stakeholders have the attributes of legitimacy and power, their impact within the organization is certain. The attributes of these stakeholders are that they have the ability to act on their requirements and have formal mechanisms that support the significance of their status within the organization, for example, non- executive directors.

Discretionary stakeholders

These stakeholders have the power of legitimacy. However, they have no rights to directly impact the organization and have no immediate rights.

There is absolutely no pressure on the organization to participate in any working association or connections unless they decide too. An example of this may be engagement upon social media forums.

Dependent stakeholders

This group have an absence of real power. However, they have legitimacy and also can create a sense of urgency. There will be a dependency upon other stakeholders within the organization that have the relevant status. The power in this association with the dominant part of this association, an example is employees of the organization.

Demanding stakeholders

This will occur when there is a single driver in place: urgency. This will exclude any legitimacy or direct influences upon the organization.

This stakeholder type may be irritating and potentially exasperating. However, they may not warrant more than passing engagement or attention. For example, a supplier continually demanding payment or threating legal action outside agreed contracted terms.

Dangerous stakeholders

This occurs when the stakeholder has power and can create a level of urgency. These may be intimidating in their approach towards the organization. This threatening approach is not legitimate, however it is a tactic than can be deployed. An example of this may include wildcat strikes or outside pressure groups that, in effect, use terrorist methods in creating a sense of urgency disproportionate to any legitimacy.

Definitive Stakeholders

Those who have real legitimacy, significant power and have the right to create urgency within an organization are definitive stakeholders. These can change strategy, priorities and allocate resources to other stakeholder groups, e.g. the direct chain of management control through to the CEO.

Features that impact the placement of business partners

The features of the business partner and stakeholder relationships influence where the business partner might be best placed. The range is conditional upon the number of influences that are in place, and also the profiles and features of the stakeholder.

In summary, the optimum emotional and acceptable position for the business partner placement will be impacted by several factors that have been described and illustrated in Figure 3.9. This will support an initial implementation of a business partnering relationship and also support effectiveness reviews on an on going basis. Where placement is optimized the degree and prioritization which business partners decide, and act upon, are enhanced for the benefit of the whole organization.

Features which impact where the business partner should be positioned

Figure 3.9 Conditional ranges

THE SERVICE CONTENT ENGAGEMENT

The initial consideration for any service improvement is to define and understand what is the current state, the 'As-Is' position. This, ideally, should be fully understood by the business partner before any improvements are recommended and before the deployment of any methods or models. This section is aimed at showing how the business partner may improve the service content that is being delivered to stakeholders. Efficient service content will support effective outcomes by clarity of responsibilities, process improvement, and utilizing models that are aimed to improve them. This can be described as the 'To-Be' position.

Power in relation to engagement

In Chapter 2 we examined different types of power. A comprehensive understanding of power types supports the effectiveness of the preparation stage for the business partner. The engagement of how to deal with power/ interest groups now follows. The business partner may have stakeholder(s) who will have differing interest and power upon the activities that they will engage with. Eden and Ackermann (1998) identify a method of identifying the relationship between the power and interest of a stakeholder. Any potential engagement or conflict identification will need to address and be significantly influenced by the power of the stakeholder. The power/ interest matrix method can support:

- a one-to-one relationship
- multiple stakeholders
- project-based activities.

This will support the boundaries of the service content and where the priorities should be focused upon.

Power–interest grids will typically support identification of service levels where stakeholders' interests and power bases need to be considered to address any potential conflict or issues that might need resolution. The knowledge gained from the use of the power/interest grid can be utilized to advance the interests of the relatively weak business partner power who supports more powerful stakeholders. In addition to identifying potential conflict in relation to the services to be expected and provided, the method will support:

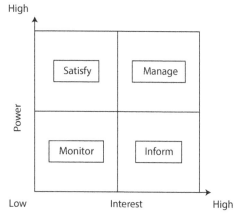

Figure 3.10 Power–interest matrix

- a collaborative approach for the priorities of the service content;
- team planning for the business partner and stakeholder;
- the RACI model, which is explored in detail later in this chapter;
- the development of a common purpose between relevant parties;
- the identification of the type and source of stakeholder power;
- the identification of common areas of interest.

The position within the grid (Figure 3.10) indicates the actions that are required to engage with the stakeholder:

- *High power and interest stakeholders*: these are the stakeholders that require being fully engaged and for the business partner to satisfy.
- *Low power and high interest stakeholders*: these are stakeholders that need to be adequately informed and to ensure that no major issues are arising. These stakeholders can often be supportive in achieving the goals required.
- *High power and less interest stakeholders:* business partner engagement with these stakeholders are required to keep them satisfied, but not too frequently that they become bored with the message or engagement process.
- *Low power and less interest stakeholders:* these will require monitoring, however they do not require excessive communication.

The benefits of using a stakeholder power/interest approach are that:

- The opinions of the most powerful stakeholders will shape positive relationships at an early stage. These make it more probable that they will identify areas of conflict early.
- Gaining support from powerful stakeholders will help support resources being made available.

- By communicating with stakeholders earlier and frequently the understanding and the benefits of the business partners approach will be more acceptable.

The limitations may include:

- More powerful stakeholders may not engage in working within this methodology.
- Where there are multiple stakeholders there may be differing or incompatible requirements.
- Over-complex analysis may have diminishing effects upon the power and interest impacts and influences.
- The level of required formality within an organization may not support the comprehensive use of the model.

In summary

The engagement process for the business partner should consider the setting of expectations and then deciding upon the optimum engagement model to utilize and then manage the expectations in relation to the power/interest relationships that will impact the engagement process. This will support the development of psychological or emotional contracts that can deepen positive working relationships, between the business partner and their stakeholders.

The alignment of team and corporate goals

The RACI model

The RACI model will support the definition of initial boundaries of the engagement to business-as-usual activities. There are several models that can align the expectations of roles and responsibilities of the business partner and stakeholders. One of the primary structured approaches to role assignment utilizes the RACI/ARCI Matrix. Both are acronyms for:

- Responsible
- Accountable
- Consulted
- Informed.

An outline of the roles is as follows:

Responsible

Responsible requires that at least one person be assigned to work in the activity required.

Accountable

Only one individual can be accountable, this may be as a result of either delivering the activity required or delegating it to another. However, the accountability cannot be delegated it remains with the individual.

Consulted

These are specific experts or end user of services or outputs. There is a requirement for two-way communication, and their views and input need to be factored into the desired outcome or service provided.

Informed

These are individuals who are required to be regularly notified, often only on key stages, milestones, or completion of the task or deliverable. Generally the requirement is just a one-way communication. These roles are then assigned within a matrix, the RACI matrix. A very simple example is illustrated in Table 3.5.

The use of the RACI model within organizations is probably more complex than illustrated and will be affected by the greater number of tasks and the number of individuals being involved.

In addition to the business-as-usual activities by the business partner, the RACI model can also apply to the projects that the business partner will engage with and support. Projects do not usually fail from the engagement of those involved. Failure is caused by a lack of understanding of relevant activities, ambiguous relationships and dependencies. Although there may be positive and high energy levels, outcomes are not being delivered to time, cost or specifications that have been targeted. The general issue is who does what and when. The detail dependencies within a project are complex and interrelated. This will be unique to each project and this complexity can be compounded by other activities or projects across the organization. There are methods that can support the activity or delivery of this (Costello, 2012).

Table 3.5 RACI matrix

RACI matrix	Task	Responsible	Accountable	Consulted	Informed
Functional director	1		✓		
Business partner	2	✓			
Stakeholder A	3			✓	
Stakeholder B	4			✓	
Business partner	5	✓			
Stakeholder C	6				✓
Stakeholder A	7	✓			

There are a variety of models that can be applied to setting expectations; another model is the PACSI model.

The PACSI model

This is a another successful model for organizations where the output of activities have these attributes:

- the project is under a single point of accountability;
- the outcomes will be reviewed or vetoed by multiple stakeholders;
- there is a collaborative culture within the organization;
- continuing consensus can be more important than the specific outcome.

Perform

The individual or team carrying out the activity.

Accountable

This individual takes the accountability for delegating the activities and tasks of the performer and takes ownership of the output or outcome required.

Control

This role can reject or stop the tasks, activities, or the project in total.

Suggest

These are subject matter experts, and can be either an individual or a function e.g. the legal department. This role does not have the authority to stop the tasks, activities, or the project in total.

Informed

These are individuals that need to be updated on the progress of the project.

Efficient and effective practice and its benefits

The practices of RACI, PACSI, and also other methods should include the following:

1 The matrix of accountabilities should be completed with those who will participate within the project. The exception that may apply here is those who just need to be informed.

2 The process of discussion and agreement of assignment of tasks is the key attribute to create common expectations.

3 Role assignments and tasks need to be undertaken by agreement as opposed to being allocated.

4 Key tasks should not be assigned to those who are not present at the discussions.

5 Any gaps in tasks will identify the gaps of resources or skills that need to be acquired for the project.

6 In relation to all the points above there may be a requirement to review, and recycle discussions until an agreed plan is formulated

The benefits of using these and other models are to agree and confirm expectations. These may include:

1 there is confirmation of the responsibility and accountability for all the key activities;

2 the of risk of gaps, overlaps and confusions are mitigated;

3 improvement in the efficiency and effectiveness of the team;

4 identification of any resource gaps or weaknesses;

5 support of the development of more sophisticated planning tools, e.g. use of Gantt charts and six-sigma;

6 support of both cross-functional and matrix methods of working;

7 definition and alignment of behaviours to the ways of working.

Having common expectations and common purpose for the business partner and stakeholders is a key attribute for the contractual stage of the business-partnering model. If there is a divergence of expectations, any contract is strained or subject to dispute. Joint expectations are often mutually met when the following conditions are met:

- acceptance upon the overall aims
- joint control of how to achieve them
- creating a win–win proposition
- engaging on a positive rational basis
- avoiding negative emotions in discussions
- seeking resolutions of any differences quickly.

The business partnering relationships within matrix frameworks

Command and control, or one-to-one relationships have clear boundaries. With matrix relationships, the control boundaries can become increasingly blurred and potentially confusing. Business partners with divided loyalties might begin to feel pressure to choose one stakeholder or function over another, and this can impact upon the power and emotional dynamic in the workplace. Within a matrix framework the business partner should deploy the following techniques to either enhance the advantages or mitigate the disadvantages that might apply. This will support the development of a formal or informal contractual relationship with all of the key relevant functional and stakeholder parties.

What is matrix management?

Matrix management can be defined as a system of managing relationships or organizations through two or more reporting relationships. The role of the business partner will operate within a matrix relationship through two primary methods.

The two primary methods for business partnering are:

1 *The business partner remains functionally insourced:* The business partner remains and directly reports to a line manger within their functional sphere of influence and then provides support to individuals, functions, or organizations.
2 *The business partner is placed outside their function:* The business partner does not directly report to a line manager within their functional expertise. They report directly to individuals outside their function, however there remains an indirect link to their originating function.

Both methods are successful models to support the service content that will be required. This will be critically dependent upon the organizational outcomes required, the levels of control required, style of business partnering, culture and levels of trust within an organization.

Matrix management will be affected by several of the following attributes:

- the organizational structure is complex;
- there are interdependencies between individuals and functions;
- there is a collaborative culture that requires mutual trust;
- tit may apply to ongoing working relationships or be project based;
- the overall outcomes are commonly known and agreed.

A significant number of business partners will operate within a matrix framework and they will need to manoeuvre to contribute within cross-functional work teams to continually identify the service content requirements.

Advantages and disadvantages

Before focusing upon creating value for their stakeholders, the business partner will need to become aware and acknowledge the inherent advantages and disadvantages of matrix management.

Advantages

The advantages of matrix management that will support effective business partnering are:

- scarce resources can be utilized more efficiently and experts shared;
- business partners are in contact with many stakeholders;
- information flows both up and across throughout the organization;
- expectations are more coherently understood and agreed;
- products and projects are formally coordinated across stakeholders;
- the speed of acceptance of the decision process is improved;
- conflicting goals can be mitigated;
- different departments work towards accomplishing a common goal;
- organizational outcomes are better understood.

Disadvantages

The disadvantages of matrix management in relation to effective business partnering, are:

- perceived dual authority or control may cause conflict or confusion between business partners, stakeholders, and senior functional management;
- the sharing of business partners may cause disagreements between stakeholders;
- complexity of relationships is increased due to the differing service content requirements;
- internal conflicts may increase rather than decrease;
- competition for resources may cause hostility within the organization when they are scarce, e.g. where the physical location of business partner is in relation to the stakeholders they support.

Improving service delivery within a matrix framework

An initial starting point for defining the service delivery requirement or setting expectations will be based upon the business partner's original professional function. This will then support the aims being aligned within a matrix framework. In addition the business partner will need to proactively influence:

1 *The determination of the outputs and outcomes required:* Problems arise within a matrix framework when stakeholders are at variance over functional goals, plans, and priorities. When priorities diverge, functional and stakeholder managers will begin to compete for resources and power. This includes competition for services that are scarce. Clear and early objective setting will help mitigate this.
2 *The setting of priorities:* Managers working within the matrix structure will need to coordinate and synchronize their priorities to minimize conflicts

and also understand the power and political differences between 'solid' and 'dotted' line reporting. The business partner will need to identify any conflicting priorities and could act as a facilitating influence upon this.

3   *The effectiveness of meetings:* Organizations adopting the matrix structure should recognize and support that the success of meetings is dependent upon interpersonal, communication and conflict resolution skills. This should be planned as a recurring part of the working relationship, rather than reacting to events. A preventative schedule will support the organization to operate more efficiently and effectively. The business partner can support this by supporting efficient agenda setting, meeting behaviours, and supporting the closure of any emerging conflicts.

4   *Communication:* The word communication has its root in the Latin word *communicare* meaning 'to share'. Given the potential for conflict caused by any dual command or reporting structures, there is a requirement for regular communication. The business partner should proactively and consistently share ideas, views, issues, opportunities, and risks with all key parties. This sharing is what will create value to both the stakeholders and functional management.

In summary, the business partner needs to be aware that, even when an organization does not label its structure as a matrix framework of management system or is defined within an organization chart, there may be an implicit matrix structure. When employees are grouped into work teams that are led by someone other than their primary manager, it is a matrix relationship.

Chapter summary

In summary, to engage is to occupy or attract someone's attention. The requirement for effective engagement will include the importance of setting expectations and dealing with any initial conflicts. The models and their features that may be used for in-depth engagement. The factors that influence where the business partner may be also optimally positioned. The consideration and complexities of working with matrix relationships will influence the business partner working methods and aims to create enterprise value. There is a requirement to understand the complexity of engagement on a multi-dimensional level and the different models that might be adopted will influence the style of engagement. Effective engagement should also consider the impact on the softer issues that will build and support effective relationships. Working in a matrix relationship for the business partner in some form is probable. Therefore understanding of legitimacy, urgency, power, and how this impacts the relationship then may become a critical component of effective engagement.

In Chapter 4 the acceptance stage is covered, which will include how to deal with conflict, methods and models of acceptance and then full integration of the business partner.

References

Costello T. (2012) 'RACI: getting projects unstuck', *IT Professional*, 14 (2): 64– 66.

Doran, George T. (1981) 'There's a S. M. A. R. T. way to write management goals and objectives', *Management Review* (AMA Forum), November, 35–36.

Drucker, P. (1955) *The Practice of Management*, London: Heinemann.

Eden, C. & Ackermann, F. (1998) *Making Strategy: The Journey of Strategic Management*, London: Sage.

Mitchell, R. K., Agle, B. R. & Wood, D. J. (1997) 'Toward a theory of stakeholder identification and salience: defining the principle of who and what really counts', *The Academy of Management Review*, 22(4): 853-886.

Stiehm, Hicks J. & Townsend, Nicholas W. (2002). *The U.S. Army War College: Military Education in a Democracy*. Philadelphia, PA: Temple University Press.

Thompson, J. & Hart, D. (2006) 'Psychological contracts: a nano-level perspective on social contract theory', *Journal of Business Ethics*, 68(3): 229–241.

4 The acceptance stage

Accept: To consent to receive or undertake something offered.
Oxford Dictionaries Online

Mindfulness is the aware, balanced acceptance of present experience. It isn't more complicated than that.

Sylvia Boorstein

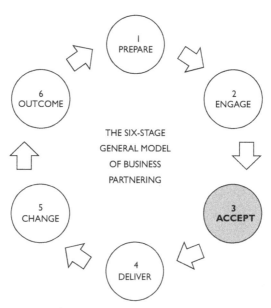

Figure 4.1 Acceptance overview

This chapter reflects upon the management of conflict, acceptance and integration issues that business partners face.

Knowledge components considered within this chapter

Conflict

- the causes and types of conflict
- personality conflicts and resolving them
- management models and approaches to conflict.

Acceptance

- the nine-position model of acceptance
- the acceptance of different thinking styles
- acceptance of the business partner.

Type
Conflict

Pg 75–82

Integration

- the integration of the business partner to a team
- the integration and development of high-performing team m
- the integration of the stakeholder's team with the organizatio...

CONFLICT

Before acceptance and final integration can take place, both interpersonal and organization conflicts may occur. Conflict is a position or state that the business partner or stakeholder will, under normal circumstances, wish to avoid. Yet the dilemma is that it can very rarely be avoided. Although conflict cannot be avoided, the approach, style and methods of resolution are free choices by both parties. Although conflicts occur, there are positive traits and models that will facilitate earlier resolution. The process and methods of acceptance will support the integration of team norms for all team members. In any conflicted position both parties are part of the initial problem and also the on-going solution towards integrated acceptance.

The causes and types of conflict

Definitions of conflict

The business partner may always have a degree of conflict with stakeholders, albeit it may be small in scope and nature. It need not always be negative, for example a differing approach or differing objectives. If the relationship develops positively the degree and impact of conflict will be minimized and this is the key to achieving common purpose in achieving joint aims and objectives. So we commence with definitions of conflict, their sources, and what the primary causes of them are.

An example of the definition of conflict includes 'The fight, a struggle, the clashing of opposed principles' (Oxford Popular English Dictionary).

We have now briefly considered that conflict is unavoidable between two parties and we have also placed a definition upon conflict. Within the business partner/stakeholder relationship there will be two primary sources for conflict, and these are organizational and interpersonal.

Sources and causes of conflict

There will be a diversity of organizational conflict from multiple sources (Rahim, 2002).

Organizational conflict examples:

1 *Changing circumstances:* The previous chapter explained and defined the VUCA concept. In a volatile, uncertain, changing and ambiguous global environment, confusion and lack of clarity and conflict can occur.
2 *Different targets:* When there are no real common purposes of aims, objectives or targets and these differ between parties, then conflict may occur.
3 *Differing priorities:* These are dissimilar to having different goals. There may be agreement upon the goals that are required. However, if one stakeholder perceives that they have a higher priority over another stakeholder, and they are not in agreement, there is a source of conflict to be resolved.
4 *Resource allocation:* Conflict can occur when there is a shortage of scarce resources. If objectives that need to be achieved are being critically constrained, this will create tension.

Interpersonal conflict examples:

1 *Behavioural:* One party holds behavioural preferences that are incompatible with another party.
2 *Divergent personal values:* The test here is that core values may be difficult to compromise and agree on. An example of this may be by differing professional ethics and personal morals.
3 *Opposing styles:* Business partners and stakeholders may have different styles. These may include different styles of thinking, communication, and working methods.
4 *Personality conflicts:* Individuals will have differing personalities due to a variety of individual factors. These will create a source of different and strong viewpoints.

Where both organizational and interpersonal conflict sources overlap simultaneously there is a risk of severe conflict. Logical and emotional issues are likely to become intertwined and the conflict will become more acute.

Figure 4.2 Severe conflict

Conflict is a normal part of personal life and also occurs within professional roles that are performed within organizations. Conflict should not be avoided; it simply needs to be dealt with, in a timely, proportional, amicable, and professional basis. Each conflict situation can have negative, neutral or positive outcomes. The business partner's core skill requirement should include the recognition, review and resolution of potential conflict situations. When it is embraced as a leadership or creative opportunity it can support the transformation of conflict into positive working relationships and outcomes.

Proactive engagement and respect for emerging different perspectives and opinions will reduce the incidence of negative and potential damaging relationships.

A positive approach, therefore, will support the aim of improving joint learning for the business partners and their stakeholders for the benefit for their organization. How to approach potential personality conflicts are explored in the next section.

Personality conflicts and resolving them

A context of conflict

Because of the continuing pace of advances in technology and use of social media, the ability to directly deal with people is becoming increasingly more important. The ability of business partners to handle conflict in an effective and productive way is a challenging, yet a rewarding competence to master. John D. Rockefeller in setting up the Standard Oil Company stated 'The ability to deal with people is a purchasable commodity as sugar or coffee, and I will pay more for that ability than for any other under the sun' (attributed in Carnegie, 1936). Personality clashes within organizations are a natural occurrence. However, if they escalate to unreasonable levels and are not dealt with they can lead to both negative personal and organizational consequences, these may include:

- increasing stress levels;
- a focus on the next personal conflict rather the organizational outcomes jointly required;
- poor engagement or depression;
- mental strain;
- efficiency and effectiveness are impeded.

There are several factors that the business partner should consider in relation to personality conflicts. There is no single personality type which is considered the best. An individual personality is not necessarily a normal or perfect one, including your own.

Types of personal conflict

It is imperative for the business partner to continually focus on the fact that they cannot control the behaviour of other people. However, they are in control of their own behaviour and also how they react to others. Personality conflicts can be classified into three types:

- aggressive
- passive
- assertive.

Aggressive responses

These are easily identified through negative behaviours that may include elements of cynicism, arrogance, irritability, complaints and negative attitudes. These, on occasion, are undertaken in public.

Passive responses

These may manifest themselves in more subtle ways and can be more difficult to identify, and may include withdrawing from colleagues and not engaging with the team personally or upon the team outcomes and expectations that are required.

Assertive responses

These involve diffusing the personality conflicts by dealing with the issues that need to be addressed both personally and professionally. The key skill and competence for the business partner is to move any conflicts that are currently unresolved into a level of mutual assertiveness where the real substantive issues are dealt with and without emotional issues being attached to them.

The assertive process ✗

The approach to any conflict in business partner and stakeholder situations should be from the viewpoint of supporting the targets that are required with an evidential and logical basis. There then should be fewer impediments with regard to resolving any potential or real conflicts. The positive way to avoid conflict is to help those around the business partner achieve their objectives. Various methods and techniques will support assertive responses to personality conflicts and some of these are described below. There are three stages to the resolution of personality conflicts that need to be considered and these are preparation, discussion and closure.

The first stage: prepare

For a discussion in relation to any conflicts, it is best prepared for, rather than taking any immediate reaction.

- *The opportunities within conflict:* Each conflict provides an opportunity in enhancing personal knowledge and skills acquisition. When there are different perspectives or strong viewpoints, there is an opportunity to improve negotiation skills, and also to deepen respect for different valid viewpoints. Effective and competent business partners will look for the upside in all differing opinions and seek these as positive opportunities, rather than risks to be avoided, as this would create a passive response to conflict.
- *Speed balanced with proportionality:* Conflict resolution and discussions are best dealt with as soon as is practicable. If a conflict does occur, the impact of this is likely to be reduced by a prompt and proportional response. However, in some instances and occurrences, the business partner may require more time to reflect than an immediate response.
- *Analyse and reflect upon the situation:* A comprehensive understanding of the issues and elements within a personality clash will support earlier closure. Identifying the triggers of the conflict will support insights for enhanced mutual cooperation on a more positive and productive basis. An initial consideration may be to deconstruct the conflict that has arisen into the logical, emotional and behavioural elements. This will support an assertive approach. It is important to reflect upon the motivations of the individual within the conflict. It is essential to understand both your own and the others motivations prior to any final closure.

The second stage: discussion

Discussion in resolving conflict can be difficult and possibly stressful. The approaches below will support an assertive approach.

- *Focus and importance:* Where there is a key issue to be resolved, focus upon this. Where there are less important and trivial issues these can be deferred. A focus on one significant issue is more productive than a list of ten trivial issues. Avoid conflict for the sake of conflict on less important issues.
- *Factual rather than emotional:* Where appropriate, factual documents should be used to support and clarify the discussions, these could include: personal objectives, job descriptions, delegations of authority, budgets, business plans, and organizational mission, vision and value statements etc. Moving the discussions to logical and factual references will help differentiate, mitigate and isolate the emotional issues that may still be outstanding and are required to be addressed.
- *Be personable, professional and calm:* When negotiating issues in relation to a personality conflict, being composed will support all parties to stay attentive to the issues that need resolution. No one listens when both parties aggressively shout at each other. Being calm, mature and personable will create an environment of listening to each other.
- *Use of neutral language:* The style of communication that is used is critical. Different words can have entirely different meanings and context for individuals, functions, organizations, and cultures. Where specific words are of a concern, seek clarification of what is actually meant. Body language is very important and using non-aggressive postures are important, for example. standing over someone, even in a neutral tone, may be perceived as being hostile and aggressive. Neutral language and engagement will enhance mutual acceptance.

The third stage: closure

It is essential that both parties understand the next steps and their obligations to each other.

- *Seek acceptable compromises:* Identifying common ground and compromise is vital to resolving workplace conflict. An agreeable compromise will promote positive and ongoing relationships, and this is key for the business partner to focus upon.
- *Confidentiality:* Fundamental disagreements are more productive when held privately, so both parties can speak openly. Interruptions by any third party will be a distraction for both parties involved.
- *Identify the way forward or next steps:* To leave any difficult discussions of this nature in a state of ambiguity is likely to create further frustrations or difficulties. It is important at the end of any discussions that a recap of the next steps should take place upon the agreements and acceptances undertaken. There are ranges of the degree of closure and it is important to agree the next steps and examples of these are shown in Table 4.1

Table 4.1 Degree of closure

Degree of closure	Recap, some examples of potential next steps
Completely closed	• move to business as usual; • reflect upon learning and development made; • review objectives were necessary.
Partially unresolved	• agree to continue 1-2-1s to eventually close; • review priorities that are triggering the conflict; • consider team-building events; • informal sessions over coffee or lunch.
Completely unresolved	• refer to HR or senior management for further mediation and arbitration.

All individuals will have different personalities based on personal values, beliefs, personal and cultural traits (as identified in Chapter 2). Different strengths and diversity of team members will bring richness to achieving organizational outcomes. These different insights and ideas are likely to contribute to conflicts, albeit many will be minor in nature.

Finally, accepting that personal insight and self-awareness, that you are both part of the problem and solution throughout the resolution of any personality conflicts.

Management models and approaches to conflict

The initial approach to conflict

The initial approach to conflict should consider the level of potential disagreement or agreement between the business partner and stakeholders. Conflict naturally occurs, how this is approached and responded to will limit or enable organizational successes and outcomes. Conflict is also unavoidable, however, a hostile or personable approach is optional for either the business partner or stakeholder. Hostile approaches are likely to lead to damaging outcomes. Seemingly minor dislikes can continue to deteriorate before finally leading to a downward spiral of negativity, blame and recrimination. The context of this section is to avoid a negative attitude and to consider a more personable and professional approach.

Approaches and methods to deal with conflict

The Thomas–Kilmann model (1974) defined two aspects. The first aspect is in relation to what you want (assertiveness) and the second is supporting others in their goals (cooperation). The illustration in Figure 4.3 has been slightly modified from the original model.

The model then provides a framework for five ways to engage with another party.

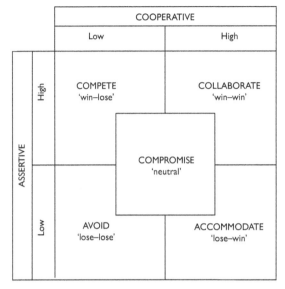

Figure 4.3 Conflict model

1 *Avoid:* Where there is a reliance on supporting each other and there is no
   dialogue then avoidance takes place, this will creates a lose–lose scenario.
   This can result in an illogical perception that whichever party has lost the
   least is the winner of the conflict. No one actually wins, both lose.

2 *Accommodate:* This occurs when cooperation takes place to the detriment of
   the aims and targets that need to be achieved. In some circumstances this
   strategy may be useful to improve interpersonal relationships. However,
   the scale of the concession made should temper this. A continuing adoption
   of this over the long term will create a 'lose–win' position.

3 *Compete:* This is the converse of the accommodate strategy. Requirements
   are pushed forward to the detriment of another party. There can be
   exceptional circumstance where this can be productive e.g. in crises.
   However, if continued over a period of time this can be perceived as
   bullying or harassment. A continuing adoption of this over the long term
   will create a 'win–lose' position.

4 *Compromise:* This is when both parties yield what they really want to achieve.
   This does require the application of both the attributes of cooperation and
   being assertive. However, over the long-term adoption of this approach
   can yield sub-optimal results for the individuals and the organizations they
   operate within. This is a neutral position.

5 *Collaborate:* This is when both parties work collectively to achieve the
   separate goals required. This is an effective approach when innovative
   or multifaceted requirements are required, for example, new technology
   implementation or complex organizational change. Over the long term this
   will create a winning formula for both parties.

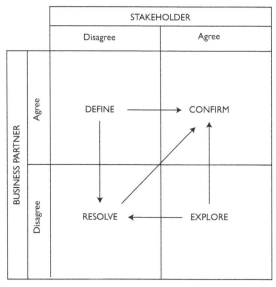

Figure 4.4 Conflict transition

The transitions and resolutions of conflict

In reviewing and analysing any potential conflict areas, the level and degree of potential acceptance or disagreement will vary. The model just discussed is useful for the business partner to reflect on which approach might be considered. However, some of the options may not bind the business partner and stakeholder aims and objectives together in full agreement for the benefit of organizational outcomes. The process of dealing with the initial conflict may not be full closure. The identification, resolution and closure of conflict are a key competence that the business partner should possess. In the previous section we defined and explained what are the potential causes of conflict and their sources. Figure 4.4 is a model that seeks a transition towards a final agreement.

Agree/agree–confirm

The primary objective will be to confirm any agreement between the business partner and stakeholder upon any particular perspective or issue. However, there may be different stages that need to be considered and then transitioned from. Confirmation of acceptance is the end goal that both parties should seek to achieve. The agreement stage may be accepted from the beginning, however, there may transitory stages from either:

- define
- explore
- resolve

- define and then resolve
- explore and then resolve.

Agree/disagree–define

Where there is a perspective that the business partner agrees with an aim, objective, goal or outcome and the stakeholder does not, the issue requires to be defined and clarified further, and this will have either of the outcomes of needing to be resolved or confirmation of acceptance.

Disagree/agree–explore

Where there is a perspective that the business partner may disagree with an aim, objective, goal or outcome and the stakeholder agrees to it, then the issue needs to be explored further. This will ensure that there are no further misunderstandings needing to be resolved or confirmation of acceptance.

Disagree/disagree–resolve

Where there is a fundamental disagreement then this needs to be resolved to being acceptable to both parties. The define and explore interim stages may identify issues that need resolution. The resolution of conflicting disagreement requires an examination of the potential root causes and methods of resolving them. This is specifically important for effective business partner relationships. The business partner may be bringing some specialist expertise and professional disciplines that the stakeholder may wish to ignore. A second example is that the business partner may be working to a set of requirements from their functional relationships.

Tables 4.2 and 4.3 illustrate when the potential root cause of potential or emerging disagreements and examples of methods that might resolve them.

Table 4.2 Sources of organizational conflict

Sources of organizational conflict	*Potential methods to mitigate or resolve*
Changing circumstances (VUCA model)	Joint environmental scanning e.g. situational matrix, PESTEL, Porter's model
Different goals	Team charters SMART objectives
Differing priorities	Refer to higher management Consult with functional leaders Brainstorm solutions
Resource allocation	Reviewing group role e.g. Belbin teams Review planning processes

Table 4.3 Sources of interpersonal conflict

Sources of interpersonal conflict	Potential methods to mitigate or resolve
Behaviours	Refer to any organizational stated behaviour expectations Refer to human resource policies
Divergent personal values	Review diversity policies Ream building exercises Reviewing ethical standards
Opposing styles	Utilize the organizational mission, vision and value statements on a neutral basis
Personality differences	Personality profiling e.g. Myers Briggs

Effective analysis, review and reflection of sources of potential or actual conflict, by the business partner will:

1 help clarify what the real issues that need to be addressed are or determine if they are simply misunderstandings by either party;
2 enhance common understanding and awareness of potential conflicts and provide insights into how the business partner can achieve their goals without undermining other stakeholders;
3 support business partners with improved self-awareness and conflict resolution to examine their aims, goals and targets and understand their enhanced personal efficiency for stakeholder and organizational effectiveness;
4 support the resolution of any disagreements into mutually respected and accepted outcomes of how to move forward jointly;
5 improve team dynamics: when conflict is resolved successfully it provides renewed respect for both parties in their ability to work within and as a team;
6 finally, a personable and professional approach is more likely to succeed upon acceptance – this is covered in more depth in the next section.

Failure to close down conflicted states between two parties may continue to act as a constraint upon the relationship and therefore may inhibit the attainment of required objectives. In summary, once organizational or personal conflicts have been initially identified and finally closed, the process of acceptance can commence.

ACCEPTANCE

The nine-position model of acceptance

The business partner will continually experience conflict with stakeholders. However, acceptance and resolution can be routinely achieved through focusing upon simple, routine and non-contentious issues. There may be instances where there are different perspectives where characteristics of the issues are complex, non-routine, and contentious both in nature and scope. When this occurs, true acceptance may require additional time and reflection by one or more parties. The nine-step model of acceptance links any latent or potential disagreements to full integrated acceptance.

The fundamental stages of acceptance are: there is no agreement, the process of obtaining agreement, and then finally achieving agreement; these can then be deconstructed into nine interrelated positions. The first three positions are preliminary to the potential agreement or disagreement positions. The assimilation position is where new information and knowledge is understood and this supports movement between or to new positions, either towards disagreement or acceptance positions. Assimilation will continue as new facts, data information and perspectives are being received and shared. The assimilation process may continue between different positions until the level and final position of disagreement or agreement has been finally reached.

The nine positions of the model are:

1   latency
2   acknowledgment
3   assimilation
4   hostile disagreement
5   passive disagreement
6   assertive disagreement
7   tolerated acceptance
8   respected acceptance
9   integrated acceptance.

A model of the process of acceptance is illustrated in Figure 4.5.

Position1: latency

Conflict can only be understood or occur when there is a known disagreement. If both parties are unaware of the conflict, it in effect hides the disagreement and it is yet to manifest itself – the disagreement is still latent and is yet to be fully develop. Professional perspectives and personal experiences will impact the length of latency.

Once the awareness threshold has been passed it is in a state of acknowledgment.

Position 2: acknowledgement

One party may not be aware there is a potential disagreement. Where there is a dominating style by one party, there may be a lack of awareness that there is even any disagreement and this may take time to manifest itself. Collaborative styles

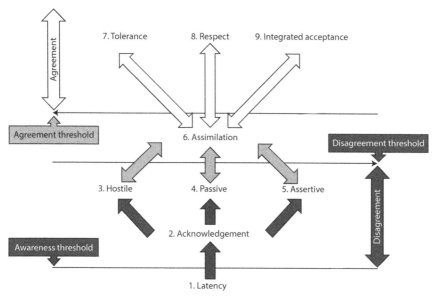

Figure 4.5 The nine-stage model

will acknowledge disagreements within speedier time frames. Acknowledgement is not the same as disagreement; it is the state of the initial awareness by both parties. Acknowledgment will occur when both parties appreciate, realize, have awareness and have knowledge of a difference that might need resolution or for a potential disagreement to commence. This will then move to either a hostile, passive or assertive disagreement.

Position 3: hostile disagreement

This stage may commence after acknowledgment stage is attained by both parties and is then made apparent to both parties.

A hostile disagreement will have some or all of the attributes between two parties that demonstrate:

- there is significant conflict;
- a prolonged dispute or debate;
- an argument that is unresolved;
- a conflict of opinions that need resolution;
- a failure to agree.

There is a strong emotional content and weaker logical thought that creates a win–lose disagreement.

Position 4: passive disagreement

A passive disagreement will have some or all of the attributes between two parties that demonstrate:

- deliberate procrastination on issues;
- disguising criticism with compliments;
- silence;
- low engagement;
- avoiding the issue.

There is still emotional content in the disagreement, however part of the logic is now being partly accepted. This creates a win–neutral disagreement.

Position 5: assertive disagreement

Assertive disagreement will occur when there is little or no emotional content in the disagreement; it is based in the main on logic, even though the logic may still not be agreed upon. An assertive disagreement will have some or all of the attributes between two parties that demonstrate:

- their disagreement by expressing logic;
- using non-hostile language or personalization of issues;
- there is little emotional content in the argument;
- using positive body language;
- persistently seeking clarification which will move the discussion past the disagreement threshold into the assimilation position.

Position 6: assimilation

Through assimilation, new information, data and knowledge is added to existing understanding and perspectives. By receiving and reinterpreting new evidence and information, this will support additional knowledge that may move the individual to a different position.

Assimilation is the stage where the individual will move either through a threshold of agreement of a tolerant, respected, or integrated acceptance level or revert back through the threshold of disagreement, towards hostile, passive, or ideally an assertive position.

Assimilation is the process of internalizing new thoughts, ideas, and facts for consideration.

In effect, continuing assimilation can support either an increasing level of agreement or move back towards a state of disagreement. It is neither in a state of disagreement or agreement, it is the process of clarification.

Position 7: tolerated agreement

Based on its Latin origin, tolerance, or toleration is most commonly viewed negatively as 'putting up with' something disliked or even hated. If a business partner or stakeholder is prepared to 'put up with' something, this is not true acceptance. Tolerance may occur when the power of the stakeholder is not used against an individual who is underperforming. This power could include the use of the withholding of financial rewards that may be expected e.g. pay award or non- financial sanctions (such as flexible working hours). This may lead to disagreement not being partly resolved. Remaining in a tolerated agreement position will have the attributes of still feeling negative or uncomfortable with this level of acceptance. This is a win–lose state of acceptance, and, if possible, further assimilation should take place.

Position 8: respected acceptance

Respect is an individual perspective of the appreciation of the qualities and point of view of the party that is being engaged with. Respect will be a positive feeling of esteem or deference for an expert, stakeholder or business partner. Respected acceptance will occur if there are no perceived implicit negative impacts upon the individual. These perceived negative impacts may also include sanctions from the stakeholder of both a financial and a non-financial nature. Remaining in a respected stage of acceptance will have the attributes of feeling positive and comfortable with this level of acceptance. This is a win–neutral state of acceptance. There may not be a requirement to move back towards the assimilation position, however this may still be considered.

Position 9: integrated acceptance

This occurs when there is a win–win position and the points of view are in balance and fully integrated, each party knows what to do next without referring to each other upon substantive points. There should be no significant requirement to move back to assimilation, there is full and integrated acceptance by both parties. However, there may be different levels of informality and formality upon the final integrated acceptance stage. The acceptance may be implied, and this type of acceptance may not be clearly expressed or documented, but the intent to consent to the presented conditions have been discussed and accepted, for example, a handshake. Expressed acceptance involves making a documented and unambiguous acceptance of the set conditions that have been discussed and finally agreed, for example, including these into a service level agreement or personal objectives and this may require further clarification within the assimilated position and then route back to the integrated acceptance position.

Summary

There are different positions of disagreement and agreement and where required the assimilation position and process will mitigate the disagreement and/or enhance the final level of the agreement.

Without clear closure of a mutually accepted position there is a danger of:

- ambiguity;
- frustration;
- stress;
- outputs and outcome requirements being at risk;
- time and resources being negatively impacted;
- reputational damage if external stakeholders are being impacted.

All of these may result in reverting back to a state of disagreement or, in the worst case, an additional recycling of issues, but then within a more conflicted state. In a tolerated state of acceptance there is a risk of passive resistance and this may impact upon the cycle times of moving forward towards common aims. Thinking styles will impact upon a state of full acceptance and a review of these now follows.

The acceptance of different thinking styles

Within the nine-stage acceptance model, the acknowledgement and assimilation stages will be influenced by thinking styles. Positive and negative thinking and their impacts are contagious. In this section we will examine general principles and observations of negative and positive models that can also be applied for different thinking styles. In moving towards acceptance from different perspectives, a positive approach will support the closure of conflict towards acceptance.

Negative thinking

Negative thoughts can be more prevalent than positive thinking. Negative thinking in business partner relationships should be avoided; this can be a source of conflict in relationships. However, being aware of when this occurs will support the business partner to move the thought processes and then discussions to a more positive and acceptable position. Negative thinking and examples are tabulated in Table 4.4.

Positive thinking

It is a generally held belief that most business partners or stakeholders would prefer to deal with positive people and avoid negative ones. We affect, and are affected and impacted by the individuals we meet, this occurs instinctively, initially through thoughts, then words, and finally feelings. Positive thinking can be demanding

Table 4.4 Negative thinking traits

Negative thinking traits	Examples
Selective abstraction	This occurs when there is a mental filtering upon focusing on selective or one part of the situation, usually negative and ignoring the rest which may be positive.
Predictive thinking	There is an assumption that we know what the other is thinking and move immediately to conclusions or solutions without detailed discussions or agreement.
Personalization	This is taking 100 per cent responsibility for external events that are not in one's full control and then blaming oneself for failure when this target is not met.
Extreme thinking	This is black or white thinking without shades of grey, e.g. "You or are completely correct (or incorrect)…"
Overgeneralization	An example of this is when one event or situation is applied to all future or potential events, e.g. "You always ……", "I never…", "Everyone." are potential openings for overgeneralization.
Disproportionality	This can occur when there is an exaggeration of a small issue into a catastrophic magnitude.
Labelling	This is when labels are assigned to individuals or oneself, e.g. "I am stupid….", "You are such an idiot …"
Over-criticality	Over use of critical phrases are "You must.", "You ought….", and "You should."
Disqualifying the positive	This applies a filter of thinking what will fail or is bad without any consideration to the positive options that may exist.

and may require conscious effort to maintain, yet it can provide the foundation for productive and harmonious relationships. People are more inclined to help us, if we are positive, and this is critical for business partner–stakeholder relationships. Positive thinking and examples are tabulated Table 4.5.

Positive and negative thinking styles are an important knowledge requirement that the business partner should be aware of. The skill of postive thinking can be applied to the additional dimension of different thinking styles of their stakeholders. With this self-awareness greater competence levels will be achievable.

Different thinking styles

One approach is to support the engagement of differing thinking styles. The business partner can improve their communication when they can match and complement their thinking style with stakeholders. This reduces misunderstanding and potential conflict.

Table 4.5 Positive thinking traits

Positive thinking traits	Examples
Win–win	There are no limits to identifying and seeking potential demonstrable win–win situations.
Balance	In many instances compromise requires the balance of views and jointly optimizing the way forward.
Awareness	Be aware that all the facts, information, experiences may be limited by one perspective; shared awareness may provide a more complete view.
Perspective	Expert power comes from within: to stand back and reflect at issues and problems from different viewpoints to find positive outcomes for all relevant parties.
Rational	Using and sharing rational facts and evidence supports effective sharing in a non-confrontational basis. Rational effectiveness is then becomes the measure of truth.
Gratitude	Now is always the moment of personal power to say thank you and show immediate appreciation.
Visualization	The world is what you think it is and energy flows to where that attention is. Many sports people and teams train to use visualizations to think positively towards their goals.

Robert Bramson (1994) has identified five methods of how individuals think, which are used the most frequently. These are the styles of:

- analyst thinkers
- idealist thinkers
- pragmatist thinkers
- realist thinkers
- synthesist thinkers.

Analyst thinkers

This style include a data and evidential approach, they rely on interpretive skills on the information presented to them. To positively engage with this style these attributes should be considered:

- correctness
- source of data
- quantitative analysis
- comprehensiveness
- systematic approach
- potential and preferred options.

Analytical thinking will seek quantitative measurement that will impact the organization.

Idealist thinkers

This style has a significantly different approach to the analytical style. Where analyst thinkers seek quantitative analysis, the idealists will seek and look for qualitative issues.

Idealist engagement should consider these attributes:

* sustainability
* green issues
* community spirit
* quality
* customer service.

Pragmatist thinkers

This style is flexible in its approach, engaging positively with this group will include:

* short termism
* quick returns
* adaptability to new ideas
* working within the constraints and resources that are currently available.

Realist thinkers

Realistic thinkers will rely on their sensing skills upon the information presented to them. To positively engage with this style these attributes should be considered:

* seeking executive summaries without the detail;
* assessing of what is wrong and a proposal of the preferred solution;
* seeking actions to be taken immediately;
* respecting subject matter experts and relying on their opinions and views.
* Realistic thinkers will feel comfortable with both quantitative and qualitative information, but it must be brief and to the point.

Synthesist thinkers

This style is flexible in its approach and see the world in opposites, engaging positively with this group should consider:

* forwarding alternative view to gauge reactions;
* listening approvingly;

- not arguing with others' perspectives;
- supporting creative approaches;
- giving thanks for insights;
- trying to close down and recap a way forward at the end of the discussions.

Synthesists are probably the most difficult group to engage with in seeking a way forward.

Summary

There is a direct link between thinking and talking. The manner in which what is then said will make an impact upon the recipient. If it is received negatively this may give rise to conflict. If it is received positively it will support or enhance working relationships towards acceptance. An awareness of a stakeholder's preferred thinking style and engaging with this will lead to more positive outcomes. Positive styles will enhance acceptance of differing perspectives and support movement from disagreement towards acceptance.

Constraints and enablers for acceptance

Acceptance of a business partner to stakeholders and their teams is a critical skill or competence that is required. There are constraints and enablers that will support the process of acceptance of the business partner with their stakeholders. These constraints or enablers to acceptance will have their roots within both personal and cultural traits. This section will now focus upon both the constraining negative and enabling positive traits of personal acceptance of the individual within the context of a business partnering relationship with their stakeholders.

Constraining negative traits in relation to acceptance

Prejudices

Prejudices may lead to a distrust of individuals or groups from differing ethnicity or cultural background. Any type of prejudicial responses will increase the level of mistrust and reduce the acceptance level of that individual. Fortunately, most medium to large organizations will have policies and procedures that will define the boundaries of acceptable behaviour within the organisation. In today's increasing globalization of activities, having narrow and open prejudices may be more than lack of acceptance of the individual, it may be career limiting and it may be damaging. The acceptance of other views and differences will support your own acceptance from that individual or stakeholder group.

Arguing

In both business and personal situations, arguments can become very destructive. Confrontations like this do not facilitate moving towards any rational agreement or acceptance, it keeps both parties entrenched at the stage of emotional disagreement. This approach is unlikely to resolve any valid and positive points that either party may wish to make. If both parties take an argumentative approach with each other, in effect, no one listens to anybody, so nothing is agreed or taken forward.

Lack of compromise

Creating a win–lose situation when there is inability to compromise will create a level of dissatisfaction in one party. Disagreements and conflict are a fundamental part of business and personal situations and they are inevitable. Compromise can demonstrate the competence of personal and professional maturity. Mutual respect creates a sense of common purpose and teamwork. Compromise is the method which allows both parties over a particular constraint or differing viewpoint to move on positively.

Negative thinking

Continuing negative thinking will impact acceptance of the individual. The scope and context of negative thinking has been explored earlier.

Enabling positive traits for acceptance

Calmness

A sensible and reasonable approach will be difficult to succeed if either party is emotionally fraught or agitated during discussions. When difficult situations do occur through serious conflicting opinions it is critically important that there is calmness as opposed to any over-reactions. Exaggerating issues or shouting at each other simply does not succeed in developing any reasonable level of acceptance from either party.

Openness

The process of learning about others, respecting similarities and differences, either personally or culturally, enables knowledge about the stakeholders are being dealt with. More importantly the business partners will learn about themselves and this will support an increase of skills and competences in dealing with interpersonal relationships.

Tolerance

We should acknowledge the differing personal and cultural differences that we all have. Tolerance occurs when:

- different views are listened to;
- not being dismissive of different viewpoints that don't accord with your own;
- respecting individual with different backgrounds;
- positively engaging with different perspectives.

Increasing tolerance can lead to process of assimilation of new knowledge about that person that lead to more productive and interesting experiences.

Talking

Talking will support effective problem solving and resolution.

In addition, the person you are engaging will be clarifying their thoughts to themselves, just through speaking to you. The discussion process, if undertaken calmly, will bring closer consensus, acceptance or agreement on perceived difficult issues.

Listening

Communication is not about talking one way. Listening to other viewpoints and opinions and acknowledging them will support personal acceptance. It is not about persuading, it is a process of remaining attentive. Furthermore, listening to others' opinions does not require any immediate deviation from your own viewpoint. However, diverse opinions can create additional insights on a particular issue. This is all part of gaining new knowledge and skills that will support increasing acceptance. The key constituent of good listening involves devoting time with the speaker and making use of empathy to try to improve increased understanding.

When the process of acceptance is completed integrated acceptance is attained, then the potential of efficient and effective outcomes may be accelerated. This is the ideal positioning for integration and delivery of high performance.

INTEGRATION

The context of integration occurs when the business partner is accepted by the key stakeholder(s) and their teams and is directly influencing or impacting the increasing improvements of outputs and outcomes. To support this, integration will occur at three levels:

1   the business partner's integration into the current team norms;
2   the interaction of all team members to develop high-performing teams;
3   the integration and impact of the whole team within the organization.

The degree of acceptance of the business partner will impact and influence the integration with these three levels.

The integration of the business partner to a team

Acceptance of the business partner will be enhanced once they have been integrated with the stakeholder team members. To establish this level of integration there are two components for the business partner to initially consider, these are:

1   What are the existing team norms?
2   To what stage has the team matured in its development?

What are the team norms?

Team norms are a set of formal and informal rules or guidelines whereby a team establishes the scope, context and the interaction of team members. Team norms can be developed during early stages of team building and development. However, once developed, team norms will impact upon new team members joining the group and there will be an expectation of them adopting these norms and behaviours. The norms may be explicit or implicit. Implicit norms are a challenge to a new team member and engagement through the acceptance stage on the relationship will support the business partner to be aware of these. Integration with the team norms will support:

*   increased self-awareness and personal effectiveness within the team;
*   construction of mutual trust and understanding;
*   building productive working relationships;
*   development of high-performing teams.

The team norms may not have been fully established and this impacts how the business partner will challenge, influence, develop and integrate with the evolving team behaviours and customs. The maturity of the team will help the business partner determine what strategy to adopt in the integration with team norms.

Establishment of team/group norms

The business partner is likely to join and leave different teams regularly and understanding the process of integrating with a team quickly will be a key skill or competence requirement. Bruce Tuckman identified four progressive stages or steps that will lead to efficient and effective teamwork (Smith 2005).

First stage: forming

The effective strategy for the business partner is to gain knowledge about the team members and their aims within the team, and commence a process of building trust between them. Challenging positively will support the process of building trust. In this stage the following attributes will be prevalent.

- an aspiration that the individual to be included as part of the team;
- disagreements or disputes with others are consciously avoided;
- openness, true sentiments and emotions are constrained;
- team members will build perspective, both positive and negative, on individuals and internalize them;
- team members work as individuals rather than a collective group;
- individuals are polite to each other and avoid conflict.

This first stage is important to make new relationships within the working environment, to learn how others work and react, and to see how the team works under any adversity or pressure.

Second stage: storming

The effective strategy for the business partner is to share knowledge with team members and collaborate with the individual aims commencing a process of sharing information with them. This will require positive influence by the business partner. In this stage the following attributes can be observed:

- individuals will feel more confident to forward their views that might not accord with others;
- disagreements will become more prevalent;
- more strains in relationships will become more apparent;
- those who do not like conflict, or have the skills to deal with this, will feel alienated;
- the team may be less motivated as a group.

Some teams get stuck at this stage and do not move forward, this is where leaders need to be supportive, accessible, and set the personal and professional standards that are required. This will allow the process of the resolution of differences that will lead to the next stage.

The third stage: norming

The business partner will positively support the development of new norms for the team. The team will support each other on their aims, goals and targets that are agreed and accepted. In this stage the following attributes can be expected:

- focus on working together as a team, as opposed to a collective of individuals working in isolation;
- individuals will be more flexible in treating the ideas and inputs of others;
- openness, true sentiments and emotions are expressed on a more positive basis;
- individuals are polite to each other and resolve conflicts between themselves;
- contentious or provocative ideas are still avoided.

The fourth stage: performing

The effective strategy for the business partner is to maintain the efficient and effective standards that are being provided and seek new standards of excellence for the team. This will require the business partner to excel in their knowledge, skills, and competences. In this stage the following attributes can be anticipated:

- the team works competently towards team goals;
- there is confidence in each other;
- disagreements are discussed openly and resolved on a personal, professional and mature basis;
- there is little or no intervention required by the leader of the team;
- diversity of views are positively embraced and also respected.

These four stages are the process that a team will go through. However, when there is new team member or leader there may be a regression to an earlier stage. The extent of this will be dependent on the norms that have been embedded and established in the remaining group.

The grid for the group/team development stages

Figure 4.6 is a grid to illustrate the different stages of group/team development.

In summary, the business partner should aim to be one step ahead of where the team might be in their stage of development. When this occurs this will support the development of a high performing team.

The integration and development of high-performing team members

The features of building a high-performing team

Business partners can support the stakeholder's team integration levels and support the aim of achieving a high-performing team. These following features will help support the transitions between the four stages of team development:

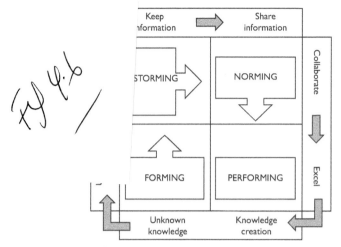

Figure 4.6 Team development

1 form
2 storm
3 norm
4 perform.

Business partners should support the stakeholder's team integration levels with the aim of achieving the standard of a high performing team. Several features support the transitions between the stages of forming, storming, norming and performing. Understanding these transitions are an added dimension to support the aim of being a member of a high performing team. The features are as follows:

1 *Help support the creation of the team vision:* The development of a vision occurs when there is team acceptance of the intentions and aims of the team. The catalyst for developing the idea for a team vision will likely be initiated by the team leader and then modified and accepted by the team as a whole. This will then provide a framework for individual and team norms to integrate with each other. If this is successfully implemented then these become the new norms for the team. The business partner can support the development of the team vision.

2 *Translating vision into action:* The knowledge of how to convert the vision into real actions will be a key component of moving towards a high-performing team. The business partner can then utilize their skills in techniques such as the RACI model or SMART objectives to clearly define who is doing what. With clear accountabilities and acceptance high-performance teams should be able to mobilize, innovate, deliver with efficient cycle times, and deliver great customer service.

3 *Managing relationships:* Where there is distrust, team members may have a predisposition to withhold their knowledge, ideas, input and also their level of engagement. Yet when trust occurs between members the opposite will apply. The business partner can support the fostering of great relationships that feel positive for all the team. They can become the role model.

4 *Trust:* Positive relationships with one another will develop into deepening of trust. This is required for efficient and effective teamwork. Without any additional risk taking, trust that can accelerate the business attainment of goals and targets. Without mutual trust the team may become stale and mediocre in its aspirations.

5 *Winning hearts and minds:* Winning both hearts and minds by intellectual and emotional commitment will deliver enhanced outcomes for all the team. The foundation of committed teamwork is more than techniques and methods that can be just obtained from books, including this one; it is also the personal commitments that come from inside the heart and mind. This combination of the heart and mind within individuals will generate astonishing teamwork and produce extraordinary outcomes.

6 *Regular progress meetings:* In the goal of delivering extraordinary outputs and outcomes there will be a continuing process of team members obtaining new facts, information, data, knowledge and insights of how to achieve their team aims. Team productivity is more important than individual productivity. A feature of high-performance teams is that they will establish methods of sharing and discussing collaboratively information and ideas on a regular basis.

7 *Continually drive for excellence:* When a team achieves high standards of performance, there will be a pivotal point when the attention and focus will move from what is working to what are the defects and why something is not working. This change of orientation may initially seem to be a negative one, yet it is the threshold that high performing teams should evolve and aspire to. Having the aspiration of no defects or errors in the team outputs or outcomes will encourage a culture of continual improvement and excellence towards world-class benchmarks.

The internal characteristic of high-performing teams

When a team is high performing they may not have the self-awareness of operating at this standard. Sharing benchmarking information and data with the team will increase their awareness. What does it feel like from an inside perspective? This will help support the validation of the degree and level of integration. The integrated characteristics of a high performing team now follow:

The perspective within the team

• clear goals for everyone within the team e.g. using the methodology of SMART objectives – these should have individual and professional significance for the team to support the aims and goal congruence of the team;

- clear roles are important to support team outputs and outcomes, e.g. utilizing the RACI model will support this;
- effective decision-making based on quantitative and qualitative analysis;
- supportive leadership for the team;
- seeking continuing levels of improvement towards world-class standards.

Positive self-perspective and assessment of the team upon themselves is highly motivational. However, the team impact upon the organization as a whole may be a more critical assessment. The stakeholder's team and the impact that the business partner is integrating towards the organizational objectives is the ultimate objective that should be targeted.

The integration of the stakeholder's team with the organization

The business partner's role should not be simply limited to the stakeholder's team, as this could be considered as ineffective within an overall organizational assessment. An effective business partner will focus and support the team to align and integrate themselves towards the organizational goals requirements. If the team is already high performing and highly motivated, the alignment will be simpler and less difficult.

Initially the impact or influence that the business partner may have upon integrating the team with the organisation may seem daunting and difficult. Despite the perception of complexity and difficulty, there are three simple strategic questions that the business partner needs to consider to initially assess, and then influence, the level of integration. These open questions are:

1   How is the team aligned to organisational behaviours?
2   What is the organisation trying to achieve?
3   How does the team support it ?

Examples of the 'how' (qualitative) and 'what' (quantitative) integration are tabulated in Tables 4.6 and 4.7

In addition, there are outside assessments, which will support testing and checking the level of integration of the team to the organization entity.

These include:

- global methods, for example, benchmarking;
- regional methods, for example, European Foundation for Quality Management EFQM;
- national methods, for example, Investors in People.

These methods are discussed in more detail in Chapter 5.

When a team is perceived as high performing by the organization the level of integration will be high and there will be a set of common characteristics.

Table 4.6 The 'how' aspects of integration

Examples of qualitative questions	Examples of strong integration	Examples of weak integration
How does the vision of the organization relate to the team?	All team members can articulate the vision	The individuals within the team cannot explain this. e.g. 'I don't understand what this means'
How is the mission statement applied within the team?	There is line of sight of what the organization mission is to the individual. e.g. President John Kennedy once visited NASA. He came across a cleaner and asked him what his job was. The cleaner replied: 'My job is to help to put a man on the moon'. (Milton, 2009)	The context is alien and cannot be described by the individual
How are the values applied within the team?	Individual exhibit this in their daily activities.	Only discussed and assessed at annual performance review,

Table 4.7 The 'what' aspects of integration

Quantitative questions	Examples of strong integration	Examples of weak integration
What are the business plan objectives we need to meet as a team?	Fully worked up detailed plans are in place.	Aspirational without any quantification.
What are the budgets and how do they link into our activities?	Individuals and the team can explain what is required and how they will proactively manage the impacts to their activities.	There is vulnerable alignment between budgets and activities.
What are the project deliverables?	Time, specification and cost parameters have been clearly defined through detailed plans with milestones for each stage and all stakeholders outside the team have been actively engaged.	The absence of some or all of these criteria.

Organizational perspectives of a high performing team

These outside observations will also be known within the team. These include the what and how perspectives:

The 'what' perspective may include:

- delivering its targets to the organization to high professional standards;
- cited as a team role model throughout the organization;
- sharing its best practices with the organization, and these being diffused and accepted by other parts of the organization;
- benchmarking methods, which confirm the standard of a high performing, excellent or a world-class team;
- projects that impact the organization consistently succeed within their stated aims.

The 'how' perspective should include:

- managing conflict effectively and cooperatively by dealing with conflict openly and transparently with others outside the team;
- open, clear and consistent communication to their stakeholders outside the team and using effective communication methods and channels that are 'stakeholder centric';
- outside trust and acceptance for individuals within the team and also the team as a whole;
- positive atmosphere, which explores and accept new ideas, engages with all team members that creates energy towards meeting the teams aims and goals including those from outside the team;
- valued diversity with other stakeholders or organizations.

Chapter summary

In summary, acceptance is to consent to receive or undertake something offered.

Before final integrated acceptance can be attained, interpersonal and organization conflict invariably will occur. Although conflicts occur there are positive aspects and models that will facilitate earlier resolution. Both participants are part of the initial problem and then the final solution. The appraisal of conflicts should include what are the causes of them. The process and methods of acceptance will support the integration of team norms in all team members. When fully integrated acceptance is attained the delivery of outputs and outcomes will be enhanced and this supports positive resolution of both personal and organizational conflicts. Acceptance of the business partner will be enhanced by appreciation of the differing thinking styles and models that can be applied. Full integration of the business partner into teams that deliver outstanding results is a feature of full and complete acceptance.

In Chapter 5 we now appraise delivery models, methods, tools and techniques that can support the business partner in delivering outputs and outcomes to their stakeholders. We now move to stage 4 of the general model.

References:

Bramson, Robert M. (1994) *Coping with Difficult Bosses*. Upper Saddle River, NJ: Prentice Hall & IBD.

Carnegie, Dale (1936) *How to Win Friends and Influence People*. New York: Simon & Schuster.

Rahim, M. A. (2002) 'Toward a theory of managing organizational conflict'. *The International Journal of Conflict Management*, 13, 206–235.

Milton, N (2009) 'Are you putting a man on the moon? Or just trying out a new mop?' Knoco Stories. Retrieved 17 November 2015 from http://www.nickmilton.com/2009/06/are-you-putting-man-on-moon-or-just.html

Smith, M. K. (2005). 'Bruce W. Tuckman – forming, storming, norming and performing in groups', *The Encyclopaedia of Informal Education*. Retrieved 30 November 2015 from http://infed.org/mobi/bruce-w-tuckman-forming-storming-norming-and-performing-in-groups/.

Thomas, K. W. (1976). 'Conflict and conflict management'. In M. D. Dunnette (ed.), *Handbook in Industrial and Organizational Psychology* (pp. 889–935). Chicago, IL: Rand McNally.

Thomas, K. W., and Kilmann, R. H. (1974). *Thomas-Kilmann Conflict Mode Instrument*. Mountain View, CA: Xicom.

5   The delivery stage

Deliver: to provide something promised or expected.

Oxford Dictionaries Online

Better to illuminate than merely to shine, to deliver to others contemplated truths than merely to contemplate.

Thomas Aquinas

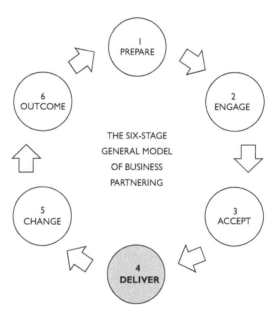

Figure 5.1 Delivery overview

This chapter examines the scope and the support methods that business partners deal with.

Knowledge components considered within this chapter

Defining the scope of delivery

- business, delivery and operating models
- type and definitions of delivery
- constraints and enablers for delivery.

Delivery support methods

- overview of support methods
- SWOT (strengths, weaknesses, opportunities and threats)
- risk management
- 4C model (cash, compliance, cycle times and customer service)
- KPIs (key performance indicators)
- budgets
- functional methods of delivering outputs.

THE DISTINCTION BETWEEN DELIVERY, IMPROVEMENT AND CHANGE

Constraints and enablers to delivery

Overview of business, operating and delivery models

The review and application of the earlier chapters will have provided a preliminary insight to the business partner for the three stages of prepare, engage, and accept. At the fourth stage, the delivery stage, the business partner should be comprehensively cognizant of the operating methods that they are utilizing with their stakeholder and their teams.

In addition they should also be aware of the organizational context that they operate within. To support the clarification of the delivery process and activities there are three definitions that will be used throughout this chapter which are outlined in Table 5.1.

If the business partner is assigned at a strategic level, the focus will be upon the business model. If the placement is within a functional operating role, the focus will be upon the operating model. Where there are end-to-end business delivery requirements, the delivery model definition will apply.

Diagnostics for defining the model type

The diagnostics in this section are examples rather than a comprehensive review which might be considered by the business partner. The diagnostic method for the business partner is to consider delivery issues in relation to the model type that they operate within, for example, business, operating, or delivery model. The diagnostic method developed by the author is explained in Figure 5.2

Table 5.1 Model types and definitions

Model type	Definition	Features
Business model.	'The organization's chosen system of inputs, business activities, outputs and outcomes that aims to create value over the short, medium and long term.' (CIMA 2013)	Applies to the whole organization. Policy choices. Explores new methods. Adopts strategic ideas to improve business outcomes.
Operating model.	A model that applies to the stakeholders remit.	Specific to the stakeholder and their teams. Procedural choices. Exploits existing methods of working.
Delivery model.	Describes and includes the business and operating model.	Links activities to the Operating and Delivery business model.

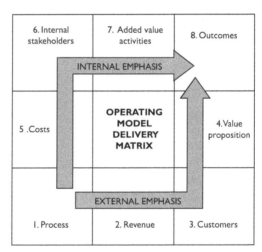

Figure 5.2 Diagnostic method

The diagnostic method will determine if the operating model has an internal or external emphasis.

The eight steps of the diagnostic method are:

1 Process

The high level processes covering what is actually taking place within the stakeholder team.

A process diagnostic inquiry to define the operating model should include:

- What are the inputs?
- What are the outputs?
- What are the defects?

The issues relating to detailed process diagnostics reviewed is covered in more detail in later sections. It is fundamental to the business partners' understanding of what their operating model is.

2 Revenue

The revenue income activities that are occurring, e.g. inward cash flows.
A revenue diagnostic inquiry to define the operating model should include:

- What is the degree of corporate revenue(s) that are managed by this stakeholder and team?
- What are the targets?
- Is the revenue stream decreasing, static or increasing and is it static or variable?
- Are there different revenue segments?

3 Customers

Customers are outside third parties that are external to the organization as opposed to 'internal customers'.
A customer diagnostic inquiry to define the operating model should include:

- Who is the largest customer?
- What are the customer segments?
- Are there any recurring problems or issues with customers?
- Information or insights on the state of the financial health of their customers.

4 Value proposition

The value proposition to the customer will include the price of services and the benefits that will arise from them. In addition to this there will be non-financial issues that will be important.
A value diagnostic inquiry to define the operating model should include:

- What are the service levels?
- What is the availability of the product or service?
- Are there any expert or technical advice services?
- What is the speed of service delivery?
- Is there any loyalty or frequent buyer programme in place?

5 Costs

Costs methods should be consistent within an organization, however the methods will vary between organizations.

A cost diagnostic inquiry to define the operating model should include:

- What is the breakdown of costs, e.g. head count, non-head count, and allocated costs?
- What are the fixed and variable costs?
- What is the cost per unit of the activities?
- What are the cost targets?
- What are the main cost influences?

6 Internal stakeholders

The context of internal stakeholders will be those principal contacts within the organization.

An internal stakeholder diagnostic inquiry to define the operating model should include:

- Who are the main contacts?
- What is their power and influence? (Chapter 2)
- What outputs do they receive?

7 Added value activities

Added value activities are those activities and processes that are critical for the outputs to be delivered. They also increase the value of the products or service at a given stage.

An added value stakeholder diagnostic inquiry to define the operating model should include:

- What are the key steps or stages?
- What are the constraints?
- What is the defect or error rate?
- What percentage of time is based on added value activities?

8 Outputs

Outputs are the products, services or facilities that result from the organization's activities.

An output diagnostic inquiry to define the operating model should include:

- What are the cash implications?
- What is the compliance to rules that need to be followed?
- What are the end user 'customer experience' expectations?

- What is the cycle time of delivery of the product and service, does it meet expectations?

The above are simplistic diagnostics for the business partner to understand why the diagnostic model is also useful for the business partner to assess the optimum organizational model for delivery. The form of engagement and contractual position between the business partners will also define delivery and stakeholder involvement. The diagnostic tools are to support the understanding of the relevant model type. It provides the questions and not the answer to what the ideal model type is.

The critical tests for the business partner to describe the operating model are:

- Is it understandable?
- Can it be explained?
- Is it simple and logical?
- Is the context consistent with the organizational business model?

Case study

This case study examines why the distinction between business, delivery, and operating models can be important. This case study applies to an operating model as if it was reviewing and analysing internal processes.

The context of the case study

- The business partner was working as a consultant within a leading global consultancy practice.
- There was an overseas assignment brief provided. The management did not understand the systems that they had in place and what was being delivered by what system.
- The enterprise was a large multinational.
- The eight step diagnostic method was used in this case study.

What occurred?

An initial meeting took place with management that confirmed the confusion. An organizational chart was provided, where, following standard consultancy protocols an interview and fact-finding exercise took place.

One person had the position and the responsibility of updating the operating model and procedures.

This is the précis of the interview by the consultant in the role of business partner (BP) and the business model owner (BMO).

BP: Thank you for seeing me to support my assignment. What documentation do you have to explain the delivery and operating model?

BMO: Thank you, indeed we need help, the documentation is behind me

The BP observed the wall behind the BMO was approximately three metres by three metres full of lever arch files.

BP: Which file do I need to look at?
BMO: All of them.

The BP reflected and reframed the question thinking the BMO had not understood the question.

BP: Which one specifically explains the delivery and operating model?
BMO: All of them. This is why we need your help.
BP: Who actually uses them or looks at them?
BMO: No one really, they are too detailed and complicated.

Concluding point. The BP developed a very high level map of the operating model, which was on one A4 page. Many members of the team pinned the operating model on their desks, it was now simple, understandable and being used to frame their delivery activities.

Key points

1   There was confusion of what the business, delivery and operating model consisted of.
2   No one could explain the model, and how it delivered the organizational requirements.
3   Individuals who were managing the delivery of the system outputs did not understand their operating model that they were working within.
4   There was over complexity in trying to define what the business, delivery and operating model were.
5   Simplicity in explaining what operating model is in place is more beneficial than excessive mapping and over-complex documentation. One page may be sufficient.
6   The eight step diagnostic method was used in this case study.

Types and definitions of delivery

The business partner and the teams that they operate within will be required to deliver either services or products. The detailed specifics for the delivery requirements from the business partner and their teams are unique to the organizations they work within, and are outside the scope of the general model of business partnering. The broad delivery requirements will span from the short term to long-term requirements. The broad categorization of delivery is illustrated in Table 5.2 citing examples from a tractor manufacturer.

Within the context of this example the goals, aims, and targets are long-term organizational delivery requirements. Unless specifically placed within a

Table 5.2 Delivery categories

Delivery categories	Definition	Example
Goals	A point marking the end of the race	To be the leader in market share for tractors
Aims	A purpose or intention for a desired or planned outcome	In five years to be the leader in market share
Targets	To hit or achieve the thing aimed at	Next year we will be number 2 in market share for tractors
Outcomes	The way things turns out, a consequence	We sold x number of tractors and achieved y % of market share
Outputs	The action or process of producing something	We produced z number of tractors
Objectives	A thing aimed at, or sought	We wish to produce over z number of tractors

strategic team the business partner should be focused upon short-term delivery requirements of objectives, outputs, and then outcomes.

The business partner should support their team's alignment of short-term delivery to the long-term organizational goals. This line of sight and delivery support by the business partner will create value for the stakeholder, the teams that they operate within, and the organization as a whole. Table 5.2 and its definitions should provide a framework of what the delivery requirement should be focused upon.

Constraint and enablers for delivery

Types of constraints

The delivery of requirements will have three fundamental states, unconstrained, constrained, and optimized delivery. These are explained and illustrated in Figure 5.3 by using a water tap, water flow, and a container.

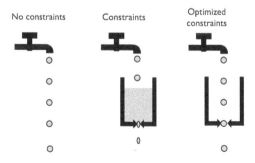

Figure 5.3 Constraints

In Figure 5.3 the 'No constraint' position of delivery will occur when there is a level of critically, urgency, or crisis. Under these conditions normal operating constraints will be removed e.g. budgets constraints will be removed. There will be clear directives from an executive when unconstrained requirements are mandated from the business partner and their stakeholder teams. Constrained positions are more prevalent within organizations and these will be determined by priorities, limited resources, and competing requirements. These constraints impact upon delivery, and can apply to both business as usual and project-related activities.

The optimized position occurs when the constraints are positively adjusted within the constrained position and the flow of delivery is similar to the unconstrained delivery position. This may include an increase of resources or requirements being reduced, or a combination of both.

Constraints and enablers of delivery

Delivery will have both enablers that make it easier to achieve, and constraints that make the delivery more difficult. An enabler or constraint can have the same original source and. in effect, are the opposites of a spectrum rather than two separate entities, for example, cash can be both a constraint and enabler. The focus in this section is on the sources of constraints, and how to use enablement strategies to support an optimized position of delivery, ideally to be in the same situation as an unconstrained position.

These can categorized:

- 'business as usual' quantitative constraints and enablement strategies
- 'business as usual' qualitative constraints and enablement strategies
- project constraints and enablement strategies.

The competence of the business partner should include an awareness of the constraints and also the ability to implement specific enabling strategies required. The examples of the enabling strategies in Table 5.3 are illustrative rather than an exhaustive list.

1   Quantitative constraints are more visible for the business partner to identify.
2   Qualitative constraints are less visible for the business partner to identify.

Project constraints and enablement approaches

Where the business partner is involved with a project, there are four typical interrelated constraints/enablers for delivery. These are time, specification, quality, and cost. Project management will be covered in more detail in Chapter 6.

Constraints, sources, and enabler examples are tabulated in Table 5.5.

Table 5.3 Quantitative constraints

Quantitative constraint examples	Source	Potential enabling strategies
Insufficient budgets	Cash	Effective business cases Longer-term planning to secure funding e.g. engagement with the business planning process
Procedures to restrictive	Compliance	Reviewing the relevance and consider different methods, e.g. moving from 100 per cent audit to statistical sampling
Support activities take too long	Cycle time	Reviewing the true constraints such as bottlenecks Prioritizing attention and activities to the constraint
Manual or part systemized processes	Systems.	System upgrades New system New technologies
Insufficient resources	Resources	These can be cash, staff, resources or materials Lean strategies to free up resources Requesting powerful stakeholders to redirect or allocate resources

Table 5.4 Qualitative constraints

Qualitative constraint examples	Source	Potential enabling strategies
Different values in different countries	Cultural	Self-education Being aware of company policies
Aggressive and poor behaviours	Behavioural	Develop assertive strategies Apply the nine-step model for acceptance
Individual team members failing or not taking responsibility	Team dynamics	Team building Awareness of team roles RACI, Belbin and performance management
Changing regulations for the organization	External factors	PESTEL analysis SWOT Impact analysis
The issue of demanding and unreasonable customers	Customer expectations	Engaging with customers Collaborative win–win tactics Customer service training

Table 5.5 Project constraints

Project constraint examples	Source	Potential enabling strategies
Tight schedules	Time	Reduce the specification requirements and/or increase the resources on the project, this could increase or decrease the cost
Challenging designs	Specification	Increase the time allowed to review and develop the specification and increase the financial resources
Defects occurring	Quality	Adopting six sigma methods for defect eradication
Budget shortfall	Cost	Reduce the time allowed, this will reduce the project costs and reduce the specification, which makes it easier and cheaper to deliver

Summary

Delivery by the business partner is likely to be predominantly focused on short- to medium-term objectives, outputs, and outcomes of the stakeholder and their teams. The short-term delivery requirements should be linked to the long-term delivery requirements of targets, aims, and goals. Constraints and enablers are part of the same spectrum, albeit in opposing positions. The key skill for the business partner is to identify the constraints that they are operating under and then, through their competences, implement enabling strategies or approaches so that delivery is not impeded. The short-term, medium-term delivery categories, and support methods that can be applied now follow.

DELIVERY SUPPORT METHODS

Overview of support methods

Business partners have the initial challenge that the delivery of services or products in a specific operating model is unique to the circumstances that they operate within. Second, there is an array of tools, analysis, and methods that may be utilized to support the delivery categories of:

- goals
- aims
- targets
- outcomes
- outputs
- objectives.

The important fundamental paradigm for any model or analysis is its relevance, use and satisfactory application. This section includes illustrative examples of models that can be used by the business partner. There may be additional models that can be deployed by the business partner and where relevant and applicable they should be used. The practical application of these models has been proven to work by the author. Additionally the business partner requires their knowledge, skill and competence to decide what additional and relevant methods to use.

The initial methods that will be examined and considered include:

- SWOT (strengths, weaknesses, opportunities and threats)
- risk management
- 4C model
- six sigma and lean tools
- KPIs
- functional methods of delivering outputs.

The skill of a business partner is to link the most relevant method(s) to the delivery category requirement. A framework used by the author is tabulated in Table 5.6. These are examples of how models can be assigned to different delivery categories. The business partner would need to establish which model would best be applied within their own stakeholder relationships, organizations, or operating model.

Each organization may deploy differing delivery methods for the delivery categories. The delivery category and method matrix may be deployed as a framework to illustrate the importance of linking the correct method with the optimum delivery category. Using the incorrect or inappropriate method for particular erroneous circumstances is unlikely to support any significant delivery results.

The optimum deployment should be based upon the knowledge, skill, and competences of the business partner and their stakeholder.

Table 5.6 Delivery categories

	Methods to support or identify delivery requirements					
Delivery categories	*SWOT*	*Risk management*	*4C*	*KPIs*	*Budgets*	*Functional methods*
Goals	✓					
Aims		✓				
Targets			✓			
Outcomes				✓		
Outputs					✓	
Objectives						✓

A final paradigm for the business partner to be aware of is that any model in its own right does not create delivery. It is the competent use and relevant application that will create this for the stakeholder. It is within this context that the following examples of delivery methods should be considered and then assimilated.

SWOT analysis

Overview of the model

The business partner may use the deployment of the SWOT analysis, SWOT is an acronym for:

- Strengths
- Weaknesses
- Opportunities
- Threats.

The method supports the alignment of how organizational goals impact the stakeholder and their teams.

> SWOT analysis came from the research conducted at SRI from 1960–1970. The research was funded by the Fortune 500 companies to find out what had gone wrong with corporate planning and to create a new system for managing change. Led by Robert Stewart, the research team also included Marion Dosher, Otis Benepe, Birger Lie, and Albert Humphery.
>
> (Humphery, 2005: 7)

The use of the method focuses on what is the primary objective or purpose of the analysis. It firstly considers how internal factors impact this objective and these are defined by the strengths and/or weaknesses. Then secondly, it considers the external factors that will impact the objective and these are defined by the opportunities or threats of the proposal. The primary use of SWOT analysis occurs when the business partner with his stakeholder has established the end state goals that are being sought. Without this, the use of the method has no framework or purpose.

An example for a SWOT analysis template is illustrated in Figure 5.4.

Delivery considerations for the business partner

The business partner in establishing a SWOT analysis within a framework of reviewing goals should consider the following:

1 defining strategic goals;
2 reviewing strategic issues for the business plan that need to be addressed by the stakeholders;

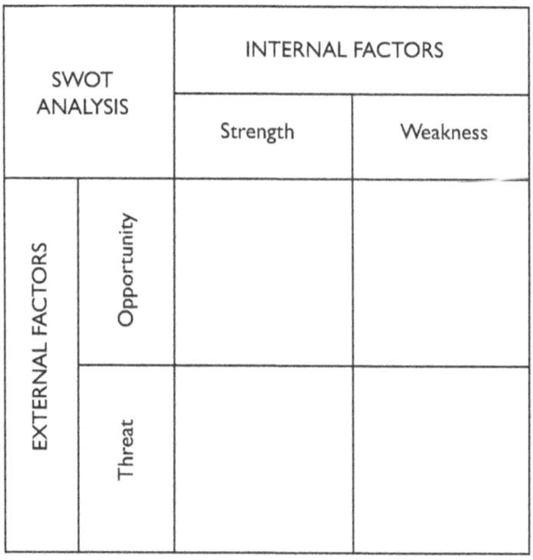

SWOT ANALYSIS		INTERNAL FACTORS	
		Strength	Weakness
EXTERNAL FACTORS	Opportunity		
	Threat		

Figure 5.4 SWOT analysis

3 additional external appraisal and environmental scanning by assessing the requirements of the present situation;
4 additional assessment of internal issues that the business partners stakeholders engage upon;
5 undertaking gap analysis that will review the external and internal factors from the 'as-is' to the 'to-be' goal;
6 the development of new/revised aims;
7 establishing key features that support the attainment of desired goals;
8 preparation of budgets and work plans;
9 measuring the stages and results in an on-going basis.

A SWOT analysis will help the business partner to prepare for effective alignment of their engagement and the resources that may be available to them.

Once clear goals have been identified, then the aims of the stakeholder can be reviewed in relation to what methods might best be applied.

Risk management

The drivers for risk measurement

In assessing risk the business partner will consider several key fundamental issues that need to be considered and these are rewards, attitudes, behaviours, and finally measurement. The rewards, attitudes, and behaviours will impact upon risk and how it might be measured (Figure 5.5).

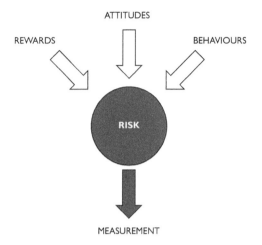

Figure 5.5 Aims and risks

Rewards

The seeking of business rewards is not without any risk. There needs to be an element of reward and risk in most commercial organizations. If an investment of a project is undertaken there will be an expectation for a business return. Typical risks on projects will be time delay, cost escalations, specification not being met, and customer dissatisfaction. A generally shared belief is that there is a relationship between risk and reward, for example the higher the risk, the higher the reward that should be sought. Without boundaries, constraints, or effective regulation this can become dysfunctional. It then can cause spectacular corporate failures due to inappropriate attitudes and behaviours towards the optimum balance of risk and reward.

Attitudes

The attitude towards risk by the stakeholder and their teams will vary.
    The various attitudes to risk-taking may be described as:

> 'risk preferers' who will choose projects with the highest risk; faced with the same choice, 'risk averters' chooses the less risky; while a risk neutral person is indifferent to the risks of the two projects.
>
> (Seal *et al.*, 2015: 428)

A business partner will need to be cognizant of the stakeholder's attitude to risk. If the attitude to risk taking is excessive then the behaviour by the business partner may not be appropriate.

Behaviours

If organizations face the concern that their people will undertake reckless or unethical behaviours towards risk, how should this be contained?

The best defences come down to five house rules.

1 *Safeguard the front door*. Rule one in minimizing risky behaviour is to prevent questionable job candidates from ever becoming employees.
2 *Set clear policies*. For enterprise risk management, key policies include a statement of risk appetite and explicit risk tolerance levels for critical risks. The company's performance measurement and incentive systems, and the degree to which risk management is considered, will also have a profound impact on employee behaviour.
3 *Create a risk-adverse culture*. In addition to policies, an organization must find other ways to foster a strong risk culture. Intelligent risk taking, even if it results in failure, should be encouraged, while there should be zero tolerance for unauthorized and unethical behaviour. The 'tone from the top' is important for how employees value honesty and integrity.
4 *Fix the broken windows rule*. Rudy Giuliani, 107th Mayor of New York (1994–2001) is widely credited with reducing further urban decay by applying the 'broken windows' theory. According to it, when urban environments are well monitored and maintained, vandalism doesn't escalate into more serious crime. With this approach, organizations must proactively monitor, identify, and discourage risk at levels within an organization.
5 *Have strong guardians*. Organizations must ensure that key risk, compliance, and audit positions are filled with highly qualified professionals.

(Lam, 2012)

Measurement of risk

Measuring risk will help support a reasonable balance between risk and reward. One method to measure risk is within a probability /impact matrix. This is a method of representing qualitative, quantitative evaluations, and the impact of them in the event of a particular risk being experienced. Risk profiling can allow visibility of the risk profile that a team should be working within or the profile it wishes to move to. An illustration of this is in Figure 5.6.

The numerals in Figure 5.6 represent the increasing scale of risk of the potential impact and their probability, 1, being the lowest risk profile, and 16 the highest risk profile.

Risk considerations for the business partner

The business partner when establishing a risk analysis within a framework of reviewing aims should consider the following:

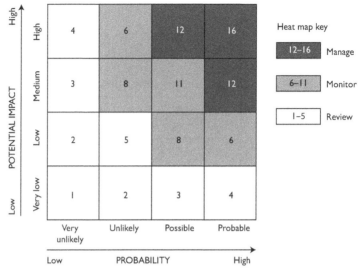

Figure 5.6 Risk heat map

1   developing a framework to review the risks in relation to aims (Figure 5.6 is example);
2   determining the risk scoring for the framework;
3   ensuring that the discussion and process should be team based, this will support a more holistic review of risks;
4   reviewing the potential impacts from very low to high;
5   reviewing the probability from very unlikely to probable events;
6   developing consensus on risk tolerances;
7   checking the understanding of the effectiveness of controls that may be in place;
8   quantifying the risks into financial impact, which may clarify and support categorization – the risks that are low should be reviewed periodically, risks that are medium should be monitored regularly and risks that are high should be actively managed to ensure aims are not adversely impacted;
9   keeping the process updated in relation to the aims being pursued.

Aims may have been identified through the SWOT analysis and these should be risk assessed. Aims are a purpose or intention for a desired outcome to occur and the targets are a measure to achieve them. For the long-term benefit of an organization, targets arguably need to be kept in balance with each other. An example of this was the banking crises in the 1990s where the focus on targets was on maximizing bankers' personal bonuses. An example of keeping targets in balance is the 4C model.

4C Model

The balance across the 4C model towards targets

The 4 'c's are cash, compliance, cycle times and customer service.

The 4C model has its initial roots from manufacturing concepts of how to balance quality targets. The 4C model can be applied to either manufacturing or service sectors. It focuses upon optimizing targets rather than improving manufacturing inputs to quality. There are similarities, however they are distinctly different. The model is based on:

1   There are four parameters for the 4C model: cash, compliance, cycle time, and customer service.
2   The four Cs can be applied to define the targets being aimed for.
3   The model can be tailored to the needs of any organization and links business partnering into personal objectives and balanced scorecards.
4   The 4Cs model has been specifically devised to focus on balancing targets.

Compliance and cash are concerned with 'what' is required, whilst cycle time and customer service focus on 'how' it should be carried out. The focus of the 4 C model is upon understanding the impact and effect that each of the parameters has upon the other three. Unbalanced emphasis occurs when one aspect is focused upon in isolation and all the others are disregarded or ignored. This can create an overall negative outcome. However a balanced emphasis across all four parameters can bring positive outcomes and so improve outputs and outcomes.

In the following sections, each of the 4C parameters is reviewed. If there is over-emphasis on one target, there is an imbalance upon delivery. There is an initial explanation of the context and then a review of the potential trade-off between the positive and negative issues that a business partner needs to consider. The paradigm of the 4C model is to optimize delivery targets.

Cash

Cash for the model will relate to costs, income and working capital requirements for stakeholders.

1   Focusing on cash can mean delivery benefits arising from:
    •   increased cash flow from operations;
    •   lower operating costs;
    •   greater volume of outputs with the same or lower resources;
    •   reducing the investment costs for stakeholder initiatives;
    •   cost and cash will be a significant focus for business partners to work with stakeholders.
2   Potential positive impacts upon:

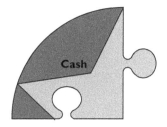

Figure 5.7 4C cash

- compliance – compliance controls are built into the service delivery requirement;
- cycle time – activities are accelerated, as there are fewer defects and errors;
- customer service compliments on the quality of service.

3   Potential negative impacts upon:
- compliance – compliance controls are omitted;
- cycle time – slow delivery of services;
- customer service – complaints on the quality of service.

Compliance

Compliance involves keeping to the rules. There are a number of different compliance obligations facing business partners and the stakeholder where the 4C model should be applied, for example, company policies, procedures, professional rules and legal requirements.

1   Focusing on compliance can mean delivery benefits arising from:
- clarity of roles;
- lower risks;
- auditor reports support a well-controlled organization;
- fewer defects;
- compliance should have a focus for business partners to work on advising stakeholders of their obligations.

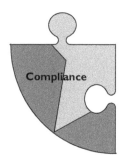

Figure 5.8 4C compliance

2 Potential positive impacts upon:
- cash – there are lower risks of fines from health and safety and other regulatory bodies;
- cycle time – rules are embedded early in the end-to-end process;
- customer service – customers and stakeholders understand and accept what is required of them.

3 Potential negative impacts upon:
- cash – costs too much to implement and administer for the stakeholder;
- cycle time – too many regulations and slows the stakeholder delivery objectives;
- customer service – stakeholder frustration and confusion arises because of the degree of regulations required.

Customer service

Customer service for business partners can relate to both internal and external stakeholders.

1 Focusing on customer service can mean delivery benefits arising from:
- enhanced reputation;
- repeating requirements for the services being provided;
- reduced risk of business failure.

2 Potential positive impacts upon:
- cash – costs are optimized and benefits can be shared with the customer or stakeholder;
- compliance – rules are built to support the stakeholder;
- cycle time – the balance of self-service and business partner support is optimized.

3 Potential negative impacts upon:
- cash – costs too high;
- compliance – rules are broken to satisfy the stakeholder;
- cycle time – too much time spent with the stakeholder.

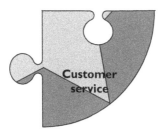

Figure 5.9 4C Customer service

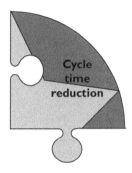

Figure 5.10 4C cycle time

Cycle time

Cycle time can be defined as the length it takes to start and complete an activity successfully. In today's business environment doing things more quickly can bring about both efficiency and effectiveness improvements and potentially create competitive organizational advantage.

1   Focusing on cycle time can mean delivery benefits arising from:
    * improving competitive advantage;
    * eliminating any bottlenecks or defects that are constraining delivery;
    * improved productivity.

2   Potential positive impacts upon:
    * cash – costs are reduced without impact on service levels;
    * compliance – less complexity will support an understanding of the rules;
    * customer service – stakeholders prefer prompt service.

3   Potential negative impacts upon:
    * cash – the costs of implementation are too high for stakeholder projects;
    * compliance – the stakeholder develops a 'work around' to suit their immediate needs and breach the business partner's professional regulations;
    * customer service – insufficient time spent with the customer, creating dissatisfaction.

Summary of the 4C delivery model

The delivery model is now complete and all four elements fit within each other to create an optimum balance (Figure 5.11).

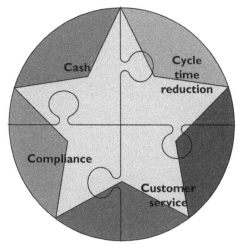

Figure 5.11 4C overview

Delivery considerations for the business partner

A business partner when focusing upon target delivery of the 4C model should consider the following:

1 that the balance and optimization is the key to successful adoption of this delivery model;
2 the model can be tailored to the delivery targets of any organization and can support linkages for business partners to include into objectives and balanced scorecards;
3 it supports collaboration within both inside and outside stakeholder teams;
4 the adoption of a new philosophy can create constancy of purpose for delivering targets;
5 the ultimate target for cash growth can be as a result of maximizing revenues and achieving no incremental cost;
6 the delivery target for compliance is that all external and internal rules are met and adhered to;
7 the customer ideal target delivery is when advocacy takes place, for example being strongly recommended by other internal or external customers and there are no complaints;
8 the ultimate delivery target cycle time reduction and service is immediate;
9 it can be applied to end-to-end processes and activities both inside and outside the stakeholders remit;
10 it can support the breaking down barriers between staff areas.

Once targets have been ascertained the business partner will need to focus on the delivery of outcomes.

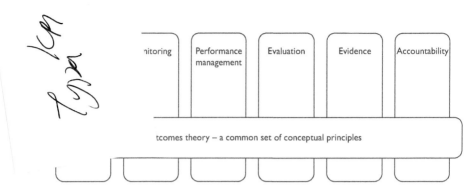

Figure 5.12 Outcomes

Key performance indictors (KPIs)

Outcomes

Outcomes theory systematically explores the concepts needed for identifying, prioritizing, measuring, evaluating, reporting on, and binding parties to account for outcomes and the steps that lead to their achievement. It can be applied at several levels, for example at individual, project, program, and organization. Outcomes are a set of common conceptual issues that link together. These are strategic planning, monitoring, performance management, evaluation, evidence, and accountability and are illustrated in Figure 5.12.

In Figure 5.12, outcome-controllable indicators have the feature that they are quantifiable. These are measured and controlled by those who are responsible for the activity or project. This means that they are ideal for use as accountability measures.

Key performance indicators assess the present state of the key activities towards delivery of the outcomes required. Key performance indicators measure the organizational success or progress towards the outcomes required. KPIs are typically focused upon the metrics deemed most critical to the success of the organization. The business partner will have a range of different types of KPIs that can be applied to measure activities that are targeted towards functional outcomes. These are:

- financial KPIs that are based upon income, operating cost and working capital requirements;
- non- financial KPIs which are based on targets outside finance, for example, projects delivered in time, percentage absentee levels, number of supplier delivery schedules;
- leading key performance indicators that will provide a predictive element of a problem or defect that may occur, for example, the percentage of purchase orders not raised will have an impact upon the average number of days late of invoice payment terms;
- lagging indicators will measure the defect or event, regardless of its source, for example, the average number of days of late invoice payment terms.

KPIs can improve the alignment of business activities with both individual and team actions. KPIs are often linked to a traffic light concept.

- red equates to the KPI not meeting expectations;
- amber equates to the KPI not yet meeting expectations;
- green equates to the KPI meeting or beating expectations.

KPIs in many instances are also used in conjunction with the balanced scorecard.

Delivery considerations for the business partner

A business partner when reviewing outcomes within a framework of KPIs should consider the following points:

1   Are the value drivers understood?
2   What KPIs are needed?
3   What mix of financial and non-financial measure do we need?
4   What customer, human capital, operating issues, supply-chain, or pipeline measures do we need to monitor?
5   Are there other key measures that are important drivers of our operation?
6   Are there leading indicators that we can develop from available data?
7   Can we collect meaningful data in a cost effective manner for each of the desired measures?
8   Are our existing management information systems adequate to support the collection, analysis, and reporting process?
9   Will it focus the stakeholder and their team behaviours towards the outcomes that will deliver the required KPIs?
10 What is the relevance of the KPIs towards delivery?

(CGMA, 203: 56–57)

In developing KPIs the business partner will need to identify what are the important issues for the stakeholder and their teams. Having too many KPIs developed and used can become counter-productive as they no longer are 'key'.

Budgets

A budget is a detailed plan for the acquisition and use of financial and other resources over a specified time period. It represents a plan for the future expressed in formal quantitative terms. Business partners and stakeholders will normally be involved in some form of budgetary process within the organizations they operate within. The process of preparing a budget is called budgeting. The use of budgets to control the organization's activities is known as budgetary control.

(Seal *et al.*, 2015: 462)

In short, it represents a comprehensive expression of management plans for the future and how these plans are to be accomplished. There are various types of budgets that a business partner may need to be directly involved with, or indirectly be aware of, and these are described below.

Budgets basics

Sales budgets

Sales budgets are the sales that an organization is planning for units sold and their value for a budget year. They detail the quantities of products or services a firm expects to sell and the revenues expected to be earned. Sales budget forecasts determine sales potential, or may be restricted by the maximum number of sales a firm can make, for example, production constraints. The sales budget will determine the level of operating costs and capital budgets that can be supported without additional investment.

Operating costs budgets

There are three distinct types of budgeted operating costs. First, sales and all expenses attributed to the sales or manufacturing process. These are variable budgeted costs that are costs that will move in line with sales made. Second, fixed or overhead budgeted costs that do not move with volume of sales, for example, rent for a building. A third category is semi-variable budgeted costs, these will not always move directly in line with a volume parameter. An example of this is landline telephone costs where there is a fixed line rental and also use costs.

Capital budgets

The main purpose of a capital budget is to predict the cash and costs for major capital purchases. A capital budget anticipates all capital asset acquisitions and summarizes all expenses and costs of major purchases for the next year. Capital assets include items that have useful lives of more than one year, such as buildings, building improvements, land, furniture, fixtures, equipment, computers, etc.

Cash budgets

A cash budget projects all the cash inflows and outflows for the next year. Cash budgets have several distinct components: cash inflows (from the sales budget); outflows (from the operating and capital budgets) and working capital movements, for example increases or decreases on payments or receipts from suppliers and customers, cash movements; and where required new financing may be needed.

More complex budgeting processes

The nature and complexity of organizational requirements may involve a degree of complexity beyond the basic model described above. However, the parameters of the basic model will still apply. Some example of more complex budgetary methods are described and explained as follows:

Activity-based budgeting

This is a flexible budget method that allows for different parameters to be used. For example, costs which are adjusted to match the different sales-volume levels that may be possible. This approach is useful when sales levels are difficult to estimate, and a significant proportion of expenses vary with sales. This type of model is more difficult to prepare than a static budget model, but tends to yield a budget that is reasonably comparable to actual results as it identifies key activities and cost drivers within the organization.

Rolling budget and forecast

The forecasting and budget processes are converged into one activity. A rolling budget requires that a new budget period be added as soon as the most recent period has been completed. The rolling budget and forecast extends a consistent timeframe into the future, this could be on a monthly or quarterly basis depending on the operating nature of the organization. It also requires a considerable amount of budgeting work in every reporting period to formulate the next incremental update. It does focus continuing attention upon the budget.

Zero-base budgeting

All existing budget expenditures and assumptions are re set to zero, hence the term, zero-based budgeting. It occurs when every item of the budget must be justified and approved on an individual line item basis. Zero-based budgeting requires the budget request be re-evaluated thoroughly, always starting from the zero-base. This process is independent of whether the total budget or specific line items are increasing or decreasing. It fully tests why any budgeted cost should be planned for. The justification of every line item can be problematic for departments with intangible outputs, which are outside the budgetary period, for example research and development, or marketing programs lasting over a period of several years.

Delivery considerations for the business partner

A business partner when reviewing outcomes within a framework of a budgets methodology should consider:

1 budgets, goals and objectives that can serve as benchmarks for controlling and evaluating existing and subsequent performance;

2 budgets provide a means of communicating management's plans throughout the organization;

3 budgets force management to think about and plan for the future – in the absence of the necessity to prepare a budget, too many managers would spend all their time dealing with daily emergencies;

4 the budgeting process provides a means of allocating resources to those parts of the organization where they can be used most effectively;

5 the budgeting process can uncover potential bottlenecks before they occur;

6 budgets co-ordinate the activities of the entire organization by integrating the plans of the various parts;

7 budgeting helps to ensure that everyone in the organization is pulling in the same direction;

8 budgeting provides additional opportunities for insourcing or outsourcing;

9 budgeting can increase staff motivation by providing greater initiative and responsibility in decision-making;

10 budgeting facilitates more effective and delegation of authority.

(CGMA, 2013)

The business partner is likely to be an integral part of the stakeholder budgetary processes with finance. The business partner should be aware of the budgetary deadlines which are required and the time needed to deliver effective budgets. Combining expert competences with finance and stakeholder input can create powerful and positive delivery.

Functional methods of delivering

Business partners who are qualified from different professional bodies will have an array of professional techniques and methods that will support the delivery of objectives being met. These should be deployed as part of their expert power relationships with stakeholders. Professional expertise and knowledge will be a key expectation to delivery within their stakeholder teams. To undertake an in-depth review of these would be outside the parameters of the general model of business partnering. However some examples from various professional bodies are tabulated below with the intention of:

• increasing the business partners' knowledge of areas outside their expertise;

• enhancing understanding of other professionals within stakeholder teams that they may have dealings with;

• supporting stakeholders who are within professional functions.

Tables 5.7 to 5.10 are a selection of examples of professional functional tools that support delivery. The web links are included with the references to enable more in-depth enquiry.

Table 5.7 Human resources delivery

Delivery categories	Methods	Potential context for a business partner
Goals	Organizational design	Understanding the organizational context
Aims	Learning and talent development	Supporting the business partners' self-development and stakeholder teams
Targets	Performance management	To understand the HR procedures that will support targets
Outcomes	Managing employee relations	Ensuring that the right application of policies and procedures are being followed
Outputs	Reward management	Ensuring that relevant incentives are in place
Objective	Employee engagement	Positive engagement will support the delivery of objectives

Source: http://www.cipd.co.uk/hr-resources/factsheets/

Table 5.8 Procurement functional delivery

Delivery categories	Methods	Potential context for a business partner
Goals	Strategic supply chain management	Understanding any industry constraints upon the stakeholder
Aims	Legal aspects in procurement and supply	The competence to deal with legal claims that may arise
Targets	Negotiating procurement and supply	Supporting the stakeholder upon critical and specialist clauses
Outcomes	Managing contracts	Supporting the tendering process
Outputs	Inventory and logistics	Optimizing throughputs of the team
Objective	Procurement and supply operations	Having knowledge and skills to deal with procurement specialists

Source: http://www.cips.org/en-GB/

Table 5.9 IT functional delivery

Delivery categories	Methods	Potential context for a business partner
Goals	Enterprise and solution architecture	Use of business analytics
Aims	Systems development	Implementing new systems for the stakeholder
Targets	Agile working	To support new methods of working for the stakeholder
Outcomes	IT service management	The identification of new IT systems or hardware that will support the stakeholder teams
Outputs	Data centre management	Optimizing the length and time of system outages
Objective	Software testing	Testing of system changes

Source: http://www.bcs.org

Table 5.10 Finance functional delivery

Delivery categories	Methods	Potential context for a business partner
Goals	Strategy mapping	To support the buy in for key initiatives and lead them
Aims	Scenario and contingency planning	To provide improved insights upon choices
Targets	Activity based costing	To understand the various drivers that is impacting costs
Outcomes	Cash-flow modelling	To understand the impact upon decision-making
Outputs	Ethic reflection lists	To reinforce good and acceptable corporate values and behaviours
Objective	Forecast	To take remedial action on risks

Source: CGMA 2013

The distinction between delivery, improve and change

Delivery is to provide something that is promised or expected. The business, delivery, and operating models that are being utilized will all make an impact. The constraints and enablers that are in place will influence the scope of delivery. Delivery is a key expectation the stakeholder will have for the business partner to support. This includes the review of business, delivery, and operating

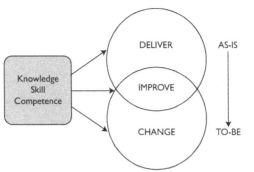

Figure 5.13 Delivery to change

models that can be applied. It defines the type of delivery that includes goals, aims, targets, outcomes, outputs, and objectives with both the constraints and enablers that apply. Within these delivery types a variety of potential delivery models are then considered. These vary from strategic goals to individual and team objectives. The fundamental paradigm for the business partner is their value proposition and contribution towards effective delivery. This chapter has explored delivery. The distinction between delivery, improvement, and change is illustrated in Figure 5.13.

Delivery is to sustain the as-is position and does not seek to change it. The prime aim of change is to progress to a new state. Improvement can either be a part of the current 'as-is' focus or the new 'to-be' model. Depending on the maturity and circumstances within an organisation, several of the models outlined in this chapter and Chapter 6 can be applied to the delivery, improvement or change stages. The application and use of any model type will also vary between organisations. This will require knowledge and skill by the business partner in applying them appropriately. The decision to determine which model should apply will be determined by:

- What is in place now?
- What is planned to be in place?
- The requirements and relevance to the stakeholders and their team(s).
- The knowledge of the delivery, improvement and change methods.
- The skill to apply the model within the optimum context.
- The competence of the business partner to apply the appropriate model to the optimum circumstances.

The next stage of the general model is change. Change is to progress from an old 'as-is' state towards a new 'to-be' state which will be discussed in Chapter 6.

References

CGMA (2013) *Essential Tools for Management Accountants*. London: CIMA

Humphery, S.A. (2005). 'SWOT analysis for management consulting' *SRI Alumni Newsletter*. SRI International. Retrieved 12 November 2015 from.https://www.sri.com/sites/default/files/brochures/dec-05.pdf

Lam. J.(2012) 'Five house rules for managing risky behavior', *Harvard Business Review*, June 13. Retrieved 12 November 2015 from https://hbr.org/2012/06/five-house-rules-for-managing/

Seal, W., Rohde, C., Garrison, R. & Noreen, E. (2015) *Management Accounting*, 5th edn, New York: McGraw Hill.

6   The change stage

Change: to progress from a current 'as-is' state towards a new 'to-be' state.

Change is the law of life and those who look only to the past or present are certain to miss the future.

(John F. Kennedy, Address in Frankfurt, 25 June 1963)

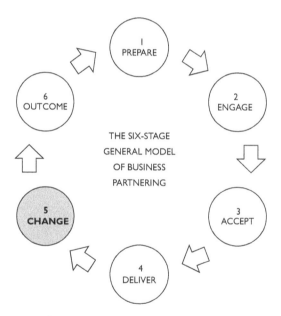

Figure 6.1 Change overview

This chapter examines the causes of change, what tools can be applied and considers how a business partner can apply change management.

Knowledge components considered within this chapter

The causes of change, why does it occur

- Internal versus external pace of change;
- strategic, tactical, and operational drivers;
- TSPM model. (target, scale, plan and measure).

Identifying change and what tools can be applied

- Benchmarking;
- balanced scorecards;
- technology implementations;
- project management.

Managing change and how it can be applied

- Types of resistance to change;
- the enablers for change;
- business process engineering;
- six-sigma.

THE CHANGE STAGE

Internal versus external pace of change

There are three states where the internal organizational change relates to external influences that impact it. These are:

- external business environment changes move quicker than internal changes;
- external and internal changes are balanced;
- internal changes move quicker than the external environment.

Arguably, the preferred change state is when internal organizational changes are moving faster than the external business environment or competitors. This should create greater organizational value through, additional competitive advantage, growth, market leadership, or innovation ahead of competition.

The causes of change and why it occurs are now examined, these will relate to either the internal or external forces being the predominant driver of change.

What causes change and why does it occur?

The context of change is caused by three broad impacts. These are defined in this chapter as strategic, tactical and operational causes of changes. Strategic drivers of change will have the primary impact upon the organizational delivery of aims and goals.

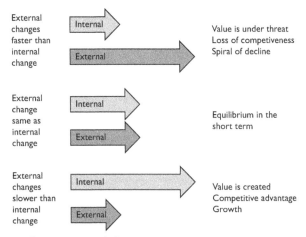

Figure 6.2 Internal versus external change

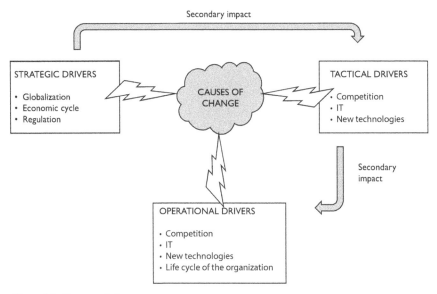

Figure 6.3 Causes of change

In Chapter 2 we identified several models that support the initial analysis of an organization's situation. The continuing review of these models may also identify new changes. Tactical causes of change are those that may have a primary impact upon stakeholders throughout the organization they work in. These will impact the delivery of their targets and outcomes. Operational changes are those that the business partner may directly impact upon their own outputs and objectives. Strategic drivers will have a direct impact upon change and also may have a secondary impact on tactical drivers. Tactical drivers will have an impact on change and again may cascade upon operational drivers of change.

The three drivers of change that are reviewed below are broad examples that apply.

Strategic drivers of change

Strategic drivers will impact upon the goals and aims of the organization. Examples of strategic causes of change may include:

Globalization

The International Monetary Fund identified features of globalization:

> Economic 'globalization' is a historical process, the result of human innovation and technological progress. It refers to the increasing integration of economies around the world, particularly through trade and financial flows. The term sometimes also refers to the movement of people (labor) and knowledge (technology) across international borders. There are also broader cultural, political and environmental dimensions of globalization that are not covered.
>
> (IMF, 2000: Section II)

These features may create new opportunities and threats for organizations and these will drive change.

The economic cycle

The economic cycle of initial growth, rapid expansion, contraction, and then depression will impact most organizations. In the expansion phase, new and rapidly growing industries and companies tend to develop and change rapidly in upturns or periods of growth. Those organizations with new technologies become the new engines of growth and may even displace existing markets or create new ones. When contraction or depression occurs organizations need to reposition themselves for the next economic cycle.

Regulation and government intervention

Government regulation can have a dramatic impact upon economic sectors. In the UK the structure of the railways, banking, and NHS sectors are examples. The impact of this is not only significant for the primary organizations but also can impact upon the whole industry supply chain.

Tactical drivers of change

Tactical drivers are defined as those that the organization is planning to engage with, or react to. These then will influence and impact the stakeholder targets and outputs they are planning to deliver. Stakeholder target and outcome delivery requirements may need adjusting and this is a tactical driver of change. Tactical drivers that impact stakeholders include:

Competition

Competition will drive changes in markets of price levels, delivery times, customer service and the specification of products. These variables will impact customer choices and their purchasing behaviours. Initiating or reacting to competition will also require change.

Implementing new information technologies

Information technologies such as the internet and mobile computing are no longer a new phenomenon. However, the tactical implementation of this technology will drive significant changes for stakeholders' products and services.

The implementation of new technologies (non IT)

New technologies are a continuing driver of change. A new technology can be described as innovations that displaces or disrupts what already exists. Examples for a variety of sectors include robotics, nanotechnology, graphite technologies, stem cell therapies, electric and driverless cars. These examples will impact the stakeholder targets and outcomes of these sectors.

Life cycle of the organization

According to Larry Greiner (1972), when an organization has been established there are five phases of growth that will follow, these create different crisis conditions all of which will drive the need for change. The five stages of growth, crisis type, and examples of the potential change requirements are shown in Table 6.1.

Operational drivers of change

Operational drivers will impact upon the outputs and objectives of the business partner delivery requirements. Examples of operational causes of change include:

Delivery targets

Business partners and their stakeholders will be required to meet or improve the delivery requirements for the organization. In some instances targets will be set without any initial specific way of delivering them. This will then influence a review by the business partner to examine the changes that can be made.

Table 6.1 Organizational life cycle

Stage	Growth phase	Crisis type	Examples of change requirement
1	Creative expansion	Leadership	More structured approach Development of managers
2	Directional expansion	Autonomy	More delegations of authority and empowerment
3	Expansion through delegation	Control	Dealing with conflicts of interest and differing expectations
4	Expansion through coordination	Red tape	Eliminating non added value procedures
5	Expansion through collaboration	Overload*	Matrix management, training, business partner program implementation Further simplification

*Greiner did not initially predict what crisis would follow stage 5. However, he did predict the exhaustion of members in an organization due to a strong requirement for innovation and teamwork.

Methods of delivery that impact targets will include: the setting of personal objectives; KPIs (key performance indicators); and balance scorecards. These techniques will be drivers of operational changes.

Team cultures

Team cultures will vary, however, positive features of team cultures may include:

- developing leadership skills;
- engaging in complex issues collaboratively;
- empowering employees;
- listening and implementing feedback upon ideas and innovation;
- and the use of quality circles.

The effective application of any of these positive attributes will drive new operational changes.

Personal qualities

The personal qualities of the business partner will also impact upon the causes of change. The business partner will have been selected or appointed to make improvements; this in effect will also become a driver and cause for change. Their personal qualities will include knowledge, expertise, skills and competences acquired through professional training. These will support and inform any changes that are being planned or targeted for.

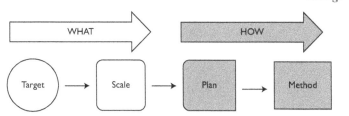

Figure 6.4 The TSPM model

Defining the scale of change

The four-stage TSPM model, developed and applied by the author and illustrated in Figure 6.4, will enable the business partner to define and scope the 'what and how' to commence change. The target and scale will help to define what are the change requirements, and the plan and methods that will support how the change should take place. Clarity of thought and purpose is a critical first step to make change occur with positive outcomes.

The four stages are:

1 *Target:* organizational change programs vary in the targets they are aiming to change. Some examples include:
    • reducing the number of hierarchical levels in the organization
    • executives becoming effective leaders
    • placement in a business-partnering role for professional development
    • customer services training.
    Effective targeting leads to the scoping, definition of the boundaries, and the scale of change.
2 *Scale:* changes will vary in their size. These can vary from a small change within one system to significant multiple changes impacting how an organization operates. The planning requirement informs the scale of the change, and the balancing of time, cost and specifications that are required to be delivered.
3 *Plan:* there may be constraints about how much change can be delivered. Business partners need to be aware that there may be other change programs in place that will impact the financial and non-financial recourses that might be available. This provides an insight to which methods and resources that might be applied.
4 *Methods:* there are several methods that can enable change to support the delivery requirement and some examples of these models and their application are explored later in this chapter. The choice of the optimum method(s) should be influenced and informed by the target, scale of change, and planning process.

In summary there are models and methods that can be targeted towards enabling successful change that focus upon:

- managing the expectations of change;
- the speed of change by various groups;
- the key attributes and elements for successful change;
- the scale of change and the choices of methods that might apply.

Change summary

Change occurs when there is the repositioning of internal drivers to the external environment. When the internal changes are slower than external events the organization will be at risk in losing its value proposition. Where internal changes move faster than external events then added value or competitive advantage will be created.

The primary causes for change are strategic, tactical and operational drivers. Business partners need to be also aware that the causes of change within organizations will frequently relate to one another. Strategic changes will be the primary impact, this will then have a secondary impact on tactical changes, and then finally operational changes.

An effective business partner will examine the root causes and interrelationships that drive change within their organization. The causes of change will be unique and specific to each organization and may vary significantly to the specific examples that have been described.

ORGANIZATIONAL CHANGE METHODS

The identification of change methods and which tools can be applied will be a key competence of the business partner. Reviews of the change methods that can be applied now follow:

- benchmarking
- balanced scorecard
- technology improvements
- project management.

These are examples rather than an exhaustive list of tools and techniques that can be applied to change.

Benchmarking

Introduction

The context of benchmarking is that you cannot improve what you do not measure. Benchmarking provides a technique to measure against an internal or external standard. This provides an insight of the performance levels and if they are better or worse than expected. Effective benchmarking may be used to support the setting of long-term goals. This analysis and measurement then helps to promote changes in efficiency and effectiveness. There are some prior conditions that apply to all benchmark setting:

- agreements must be determined about what is to be benchmarked;
- the activity requires the engagement of operational staff that know the processes;
- outputs and results need to be shared with stakeholders;
- senior management support is require;
- a timetable for delivery is required;
- the benchmarking exercise needs to be objective, factual and relevant;
- undertaking benchmarking in isolation can be sub optimal; benchmarking is only a means to an end, and it is meaningless if there are no actions to improve activities thereafter.

The final outcome involves determining those accountable and responsible for implementing the resultant changes.

Why benchmark

Motivation to benchmark arises from a need to satisfy one or more of the following objectives:

- to identify the external to internal gaps at the start of the change;
- to accelerate and manage change;
- to enable business improvements targeted at change;
- to generate an understanding of aspiring to world-class performance;
- to maintain the focus on the external environment;
- to show that performance targets can be achieved.

The steps in benchmarking

Clear accountabilities and responsibilities will need to be established for each benchmarking step if they are to be used correctly and consistently. Only then are benchmarks a powerful tool to deliver improvements. The steps are:

1 prioritize and scope what activities are to be benchmarked;
2 determine the data collection methods and those responsible for the collection of the data;
3 validate and check the data from an integrity perspective;
4 determine the benchmark and what basis is to be adopted;
5 compare the data collection with the benchmark;
6 analyse and agree opportunities;
7 actions plan and use milestones to take forward and to identify opportunities.

Benchmarking is a technique of analysing processes and metrics with other standards that are available to compare with. Effective benchmarking will consider the following: improving cash flows, compliance, customer service, or reducing cycle times e.g. doing things quicker.

There are two main categories of benchmarking that might be applied by a business partner: these are external benchmarking and internal benchmarking.

External benchmarking

External benchmarks are comparisons with other external companies using external benchmark providers. External benchmarking will help to create new ideas and facilitate a process of continuous improvement.

The advantages of external benchmarks are:

- they accelerate understanding and agreement;
- they build confidence with staff, as it is an objective method that challenges people to work smarter instead of working harder;
- they create a sense of competitiveness and a real desire to improve;
- they help to highlight on the latest practices being used;
- they identify specific problem areas;
- they provide a catalyst for senior management to use to execute improvement programs, supported by external findings;
- they provide motivation to increase performance expectations;
- they shift the internal focus from inputs to outputs.

The disadvantages of external benchmarks are:

- there are costs associated with using external benchmarking organizations;
- identifying 'best in class' or other suitable benchmarking partners can sometimes be difficult or misleading;
- internal resource constraints and competing priorities may prevent the exploitation of the findings;
- benchmarks may be irrelevant to the organization, particularly if it is in a unique sector or business;
- the organization may need to overcome internal staff resistance;
- the organization may need to overcome confidentiality issues arising from the activity of the benchmarking partner.

There are several approaches to appointing external benchmark providers. These may include the help provided through:

- external consultants
- trade associations
- specialist benchmark providers.

Table 6.2 Benchmarking

Main benchmark criteria	Impact on business partners and stakeholders
Operating costs	What are the operating costs of the individual functions?
Management practices e.g. the number of staff in each layer	Is the organization hierarchical or has it a flat reporting line structure?
The structure of the organization	Is it based on a centralized or decentralized functional basis?
Strategic objectives	Has a decision to keep the activities or processes in house or outsourced been made?

These benchmarks can have the following features:

- they are based on high-level views of what is happening in the business environment;
- their focus will be on comparisons outside the company;
- they will be driven by high-level policy decisions.

Table 6.2 shows what strategic benchmarks will normally consider.

Internal company benchmarking ✓

Internal benchmarking is a method where different locations or functions within an organization which undertake similar activities are compared with each other. The purpose of this activity is to understand the variations experienced and to adopt the best practices at all locations thereby reducing costs, improving quality, compliance and customer service. This can create a level of healthy internal competition.

These benchmarks will be internal to the company and have the following features:

- they are based on effectiveness of what is happening within a company;
- their focus will be upon comparing functions within a company;
- pragmatic/practical decisions will influence what is required.

Table 6.3 shows what internal company benchmarks will normally be considered.

The advantages of internal benchmarking are:

- it is in-house and less expensive to develop and less likely to require external third-party costs;
- it is easier to update;

Table 6.3 Internal benchmarking

Main benchmark criteria	Impact on business partners and stakeholders
Company objectives	To increase operating efficiency and effectiveness
Management ethos	To support change
Business requirements	It informs the decision to transfer transaction activities to shared services

- it is easier to apply and also more relevant;
- it increases stakeholder engagement;
- it improves the organization's reputation if benchmarking leads to rolling out best practice and performance improvements;
- a greater degree of confidential or commercially sensitive information can be shared.

The disadvantages of internal benchmarking are:

- an inward focus may result in an organization not exploiting the latest thinking or technologies;
- best practices remain unidentified because there are no processes for identifying, obtaining data and communicating them;
- internal weaknesses, such as cultural problems, leadership problems, etc., tend to remain unaltered;
- internal processes of one organization may be lagging behind other external organizations;
- the lack of external focus may result in complacency towards the benchmark process and results and can restrict shared learning;
- it is more difficult to keep the confidentialities in place.

Process benchmarking is a third category and may apply to business partners who deal with, or are placed, within shared services. This process could include comparing between the established shared services and other business units where similar activities are being carried out.

In summary to be effective at undertaking benchmarking, a company needs to implement a process and culture designed to promote ideas and information sharing across the organization.

Balanced scorecards

Robert S. Kaplan and David P. Norton popularized this concept. It is a method that can be applied to operating and financial measures (CGMA, 2013a: 38–41). The balanced scorecard has been adopted by both profit and non-profit organizations. It is a method that translates strategic vision into actions that require delivery. The balanced scorecard enables the enterprise to:

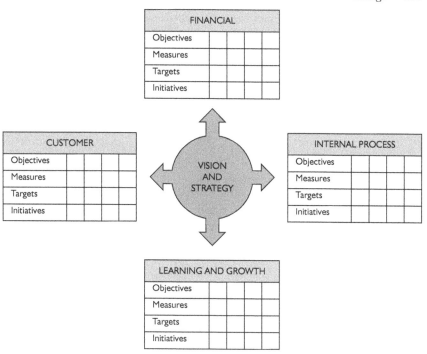

Figure 6.5 Balanced scorecards

- clarify their mission and aims;
- analyse external outcomes;
- provide feedback on the effectiveness of internal processes;
- improve outcomes by identifying detailed actions.

It is usually based on four domains that link to strategy and these will include:

- finance
- internal processes
- customer requirements
- learning and growth requirements.

The balanced scorecard links the change strategies and vision into objectives, measures, targets, and initiatives. These parameters then drive change in relation to what is being targeted (Figure 6.5).

The functional domain

In this section we use finance as the example throughout, but the points and concepts below can be applied to all support functions.

The balanced scorecard does not ignore the requirement for good financial control. Timely and accurate cash-flow information and analysis will always be an organizational objective and in well-managed organizations there is sufficient controlling and processing of financial data. However, there is a point of over-emphasis on financial information and analysis leads to a bias upon holistic decision-making. Historical financial information is a lagging indicator, which is measuring an event after it has occurred. In addition to strict financial information additional related information, such as risk and compliance could also be included. These are more leading indicators of financial outcomes.

The internal process domain

Within this domain, stakeholders should understand how efficiently and effectively their activities in the organisation are operating. Internal processes should be based on the organisation's products or services that support customer perspectives. These should be based on the unique and added-value operations of the organization. Subject matter experts who will be accountable for their delivery should design these.

The customer domain

Customer satisfaction is a leading indicator for the organization.

When continuing customer dissatisfaction occurs, this will impede growth of the organization through lost sales and subsequent declining market share. This will then impact the financial performance of the organization.

Objectives and measurement customer satisfaction might include analysis by:

* market
* product
* customer segment
* customer profiles.

The learning and growth domain

This relates from individual employee development to the totality of organisational cultural standards. Employees are arguably the most important resource of an organization. Mentoring, coaching, and talent development programs may support these.

The balanced scorecard has been adopted and then adapted by different organizations. If applied appropriately it can be a significant enabler to deliver business objectives.

In setting up a balanced scorecard concept the following issues need to be considered by the business partner. These will include:

* Is there sufficient input and support to adopt and continue using the model?

- Will sufficient resources be committed to setting the processes up?
- To what extent does the existing systems and processes support its implementation?
- Are the stakeholders acceptable to use this as the prime method of reporting and drop all others to avoid duplication?
- The scorecard should be used to drive actions.
- The scorecard may inform which KPIs should be developed. (See Chapter 5.)

The balanced scorecard provides a method to clarify, articulate, and communicate strategy into change objectives; it is a high-level method that assimilates all key measures into a dashboard that can be used to monitor the results. The balanced score card is a useful method for motivating employees. It focuses attention upon the factors that are deemed critical to change and the factors that will improve long-term performance.

The business partner and their stakeholders will need to have a primary focus upon such objectives to enhance organizational value and meet change objectives.

Technology improvement approaches

Technology is one of the greatest drivers of change. Functional professionals have traditionally been the producers of information from manual data within their function that influences organizational performance. However, this information has mostly been of a historical view of performance and was based on the functional data that has been available, as opposed to what was needed. Business partners need much more insight and influence if they are to deliver the strategic aims of their stakeholders and keep their organizations ahead of competitive threats.

Even with the use of updated technologies, looking back at what has happened is not sufficient in today's business environment; internal and external information involve vast volumes of potentially unrelated data sets. It is the use of business analysis, competences, and methods that can unlock significantly more predictive insights. Business partners must be able to contribute to providing at least a dynamic view of what is happening or about to occur. An effective business partner has the ability to cut through all data sources across the organization. Yet very few have exploited this position to gain and share predictive insights in respect of supporting their stakeholder groups to improve their overall organization's performance. The business partner may be limited by, their remit, contractual arrangements, service level agreements, data and security protection. However, for business partners to leverage value for their stakeholders, they will be increasingly required to deploy and depend upon technology and systems.

Business partners will increasingly use and be dependent on the use of technology in supporting their stakeholder aims, yet many professionals within functions do not recognize the difference between business analysis, big data, business intelligence and business analytics. These are methods that the business partner needs to apply to enhance the enterprise value for their stakeholders. So we start with a model developed by the author and is illustrated in Figure 6.6. This provides a framework for the key features for business analysis, business intelligence, big data, and analytics and how they relate to each other.

Business analysis

These are methods that the business partner can support stakeholders with. The business partner will be able to recommend options that support the achievements of aims, goals and targets, involving expert use of a mix of manual and software data sets. This will support stakeholders to take action upon activities that will make the positive impact.

Business analysis features include:

1 *Stakeholder requirements* are a clear and complete definition of the obligations needed to be delivered. They outline the specific requirements that have been provided by the stakeholder. In addition there should be clarity of how the proposed changes will impact the stakeholder and their teams.
2 *Business requirements* are statements of the aims or outcomes that are being sought. They outline the key stakeholder requirements within the context of organisational aims. The business requirements will include:
    *   why the project is required;
    *   the outcomes that will be delivered;
    *   how the project will be measured in relation to time, quality and specification;
    *   what other stakeholder or projects that might be impacted upon.

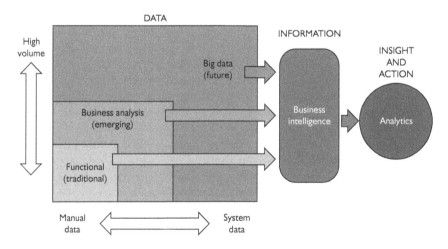

Figure 6.6 Business analysis

3 *Solution requirements* describe the features of the solution that meet the business objectives and stakeholder needs. They are commonly separated into sub-groupings for individual users, teams stakeholders, and the impact on the IT department.

4 *Functional requirements* outline the attributes, data and reports information technology that will be provided to the end users. In addition the requirements will define the responsibilities and engagement that will be needed from all users and stakeholders.

5 *Non-functional requirements* are conditions that do not impact the system to be implemented directly. These are indirect impacts that still need to be considered to optimize the solution for end users. An example of this might be to ensure there is sufficient data storage for the whole organizational systems, so there is no loss in system performance in any of the applications in use.

6 *Transitional and legacy requirements* describe the requirements for the change to take place without significant issues for the end users of the system. Examples of this might include:

- parallel running of the systems;
- keeping old data on the legacy system rather than transferring the information;
- the length of time the old system is open to users for historical queries;
- data cleansing of old data;
- ensuring there are clear audit trails.

Business intelligence

Business intelligence (BI) can be described as all the information that exists within an enterprise. This will include both manual data and information contained within the software of systems applications. BI may also not fully rely on internal systems data either. Information and analysis may be obtained and used from outside the organization's databases. An example of this might be the use of customer credit checking from outside third parties and their systems.

Optimum BI systems should be adaptable by their provision and use.

Business conditions and challenges are not constant by their nature, so BI will frequently need to adjust to evolving needs, demands, or requirements.

BI features include:

1 *Flexibility for constantly changing environments:* Organizational requirements constantly change. Hence agility, speed and flexibility are key attributes that are required to be in place.

2 *Improved Effectiveness:* Self-service and personalized reporting for the business partner, stakeholders and end users is a growing trend and requirement.

3 *Providing critical information to the right people at the right time:* This will be as a result of a comprehensive understanding of the end users, business processes, and stakeholder requirements. There are a variety of techniques

that can be deployed to optimise and customise the different needs. Examples of this include:

- reports by exception;
- reports being pushed to end users;
- self-service reports;
- real-time reporting on critical issues;
- standard monthly reports;
- daily audit and compliance reports.

4 *Efficiency improvements by reducing costs:* The majority of systems will have to be financially approved as they deliver or have an expectation of reducing costs. Some examples of this will include:

- using standard applications without any modifications;
- using web-based reporting;
- standardizing regular reports;
- allowing users to build and deploy unique and individual analysis reports themselves;
- reducing the internal bureaucracy of the IT department.

5 *Encouraging collaboration and information sharing:* Business partners can support or encourage users, teams and stakeholders to share cross-functional data and information use. This will improve the overall outcomes for the organization.

Big data

Big data is a characterization of any assemblage of data and information so huge or intricate that it becomes problematic to process or analyze it using old-style systems.

> There is an increasing focus on big data across organizations. However, unless sense is made of big data it really adds no value. Therefore the emerging challenge is how meaning and predictions could be drawn out of vast amounts of data.
>
> (Wikipedia, n.d.)

Big data features include:

1 *Volume:* 'Big data' is a term that correlates to the magnitude and complexity of data. The requirement and quantity of data that is created will be significant in relation to the relevance of the data sets, the context, and usage. This will determine the scope of potential organizational value.

2 *Variety:* The second feature of big data is its diversity. When subject-matter experts analyse data, they will provide insights of effective use that will create value for the organisation in achieving their outcomes.

3 *Velocity:* This relates to the speed that useful information can be created for the use and applications by the organization.

4 *Variability:* This is a challenge for analysts of the data. Data sources from multiple sources, systems or applications create inconsistency and complexity. This impedes the ability to use the data either efficiently or effectively.
5 *Veracity:* This refers to the completeness, precision, accuracy and authenticity of the information. Without these features, the data will be inaccurate or unusable by subject-matter experts or stakeholders.

The volume, variety, velocity, variability and veracity of information leads to increasing levels of complexity for the organization.

Analytics

Analytics is the process of detection, recognition, interpretation of information. Analytics is dependent upon the use of:

• statistics
• operations research
• manual information
• system data.

Intelligent combination of the above will improve the organisations outputs and outcomes.

The volume, variety and veracity of big data combined with the power of computing hardware and software is delivering exponential benefits from business analytics.

The features of analytics include:

1 *Analytics includes the entire data sets that are available* to create insights of business value. It was not until the advent of computers and decision management systems that business analytics really began to add value.
2 *The analysis also includes unstructured information* which because of its variety of formats is difficult or even impossible to be deposited in traditional databases without considerable resources being deployed.
3 *Analytics is a multi-dimensional method* that will include the use of data from within the function, from the organization and data sets outside the organization.
4 *At the core of business analytics is data and statistical methodology.* Business analytics makes extensive use of data, statistical and quantitative analysis to provide predictive modelling which forms the basis for fact-based decision-making. Statistical tools for business analytics may include methodologies such as:
    • regression analysis
    • probability
    • Monte Carlo simulation
    • price optimization

- combinational optimization
- time series decomposition
- constraint analysis
- activity-based costing.

5 *The insights from analytics are used to recommend action* or to inform decision making within the organization. In the context of a capability, business analytics provides new insights and understanding of situations and provides answers such as why something is happening, what if it continues, what will happen next and what could be the best outcome.

Case study: the secrets of success from Dunnhumby a renowned leader in customer analytics

Leading customer science company Dunnhumby uses advance data analytics to help its clients understand their customers better. The company has gone to work with many other leading brands, but believes that smaller businesses can also benefit from better data analysis.

However, companies need to start understanding the data assets they have at their disposal from the outset on any project. 'Your data is the place to start' says Matthew Keylock, Global Capability MD of data at Dunnhumby. 'Buying third party data may be fine for a processing activity, and can add colour to your own customer records, but is not the foundation you want to build on'.

For this reason, Keylock recommends that firms initially assess what sources of data they have available (e.g. customer contact details, organization details and roles, historical engagement data, including products and services purchased, and so on). It is also important to seek out data owners within the organization, and explore how sharing their data sources could create quick win opportunities for the business.

'Companies should look to create the greatest understanding and value they can from their data sources, but they must also transfer learning about customers across their business', says Keylock. 'Firms should also segment their customers and reappraise this data regularly to understand trends and patterns in their customer base, for example to help them identify and address declining client accounts, but to reward desirable behaviours.' As you develop a more connected data view, insights coming from it will typically challenge accepted 'norms' in the business and will tell you many things you didn't know. Finally, Keylock recommends that companies should implement data projects in phases and build on each success, remarking that 'A massive data project with the hope of some value is a high-risk undertaking'.

(CGMA, 2013b: 11)

Project management planning

The basics of project planning

Efficient project control is a key method to deliver outputs and effective change. The business partner will be involved in leading or supporting projects for stakeholders. A high level of the basics of good project management will include:

- a project charter and the quad of aims;
- contents of the plan;
- Gantt charts;
- monitoring the project;
- close out of the project.

The project charter

Creating a project charter can be a challenging part of a project. Poor definitions or misunderstandings are the cause of many project failures. Table 6.4 highlights issues that need to be considered.

A technique to define a project charter is called a 'quad of aims' and it consists of four sections to be defined and agreed (Figure 6.7).

Good practice in developing a quad of aims involves ensuring:

- engagement of staff at the highest levels;
- effective consultations and iterations with all stakeholders;
- the project team and all stakeholders understand it;
- it includes an explanation of the key features of the project;
- the sponsor approves it before a detailed project plan is developed.

An example of the quad of aims for a business analytics project is illustrated in Table 6.5.

Table 6.4 Project charter

People	*Details*	*Practical matters*
Assembling a project team with appropriate skills and competence	Agreeing what is to be provided in terms of quality, outputs and business case benefits	Choosing the best tools and techniques for the project
Finding a project sponsor to direct the delivery of the project (usually a senior executive)	Agreeing particular time specifications, the overall timeframe and drawing up the budget.	Communicating any change management issues to stakeholders
Appointing a suitable project manager to run and coordinate the project	Scoping all definitions within the project to improve understanding	Ensure those impacted by the change are consulted

Purpose of the project	Stakeholder benefits required
The specific deliverables required	The key success criteria

Figure 6.7 Quad of aims

Table 6.5 Quad of aims

Purpose To implement business analytics for the organization	*Stakeholder benefits* Management – speedier information and better decision-making Competitive advantage over competition
The deliverables Implementation of the new system Time – 6 months from approval Cost – to budget Specification – compatible with existing systems, no bespoke Real-time data analysis	*Success criteria* Business data link with balanced scorecard Improvement in KPIs relating to competitors by 25%

Ensuring a project is properly planned is a major factor in ensuring it delivers successful outputs. The project charter will be used to develop an appropriate project plan. The level of detail and complexity will vary between different project plans depending on their scope and nature.

Before drawing up the plan, research must be carried out into:

- different options for achieving the project's objectives;
- consistent, alternative scopes and options should be developed for achieving the project objectives and meeting the customers' needs and the best solution should be determined;
- any assumptions should be evaluated to ensure they are realistic and factors such as the project team used and the time required to monitor progress and take corrective action should be built in;
- the most significant risks facing the project, should it proceed to implementation, along with the likely constraints and enablers.

Contents of a project plan

Elements that should be part of the plan include:

Dependencies

- Analyses of the critical dependences within the project – a dependency is where one task or activity needs to take place before another can take place; or example, staff cannot be transferred to a new location before the office has been fitted out with the required furniture and IT equipment.

Task analysis

- Breakdown of the activities and task structure and the grouping of these together in hierarchical and time based structures – see the illustration of a Gantt chart (Figure 6.8) by way of example;
- development of detailed project goals and tasks.

Milestones

- Determination of the milestones (a delivery point of the project);
- acquiring financial commitments for each of the agreed milestones;
- inclusion of specific communication milestones.

Management

- Development of a change control process for the project;
- identification of the roles and responsibilities of project team members;
- obtaining review and approval from the sponsors before final commitment;
- establishing a process to re-test, at intervals, the identified project scope and definition against the reasons for undertaking the project.

Gantt charts

Gantt charts are a common method for demonstrating and managing the phases and activities of a project. The activities should be broken into detail against a timeline from start to completion as illustrated in Figure 6.8.

Although widely used, Gantt charts do have some weaknesses:

- They may become quite awkward for large and complex projects.
- They do not show the size of a project or the relative size of each of the elements.
- A large number of inter-dependencies may result in a cluttered or unreadable chart.
- The planned workload may have insufficient resources at peak times.

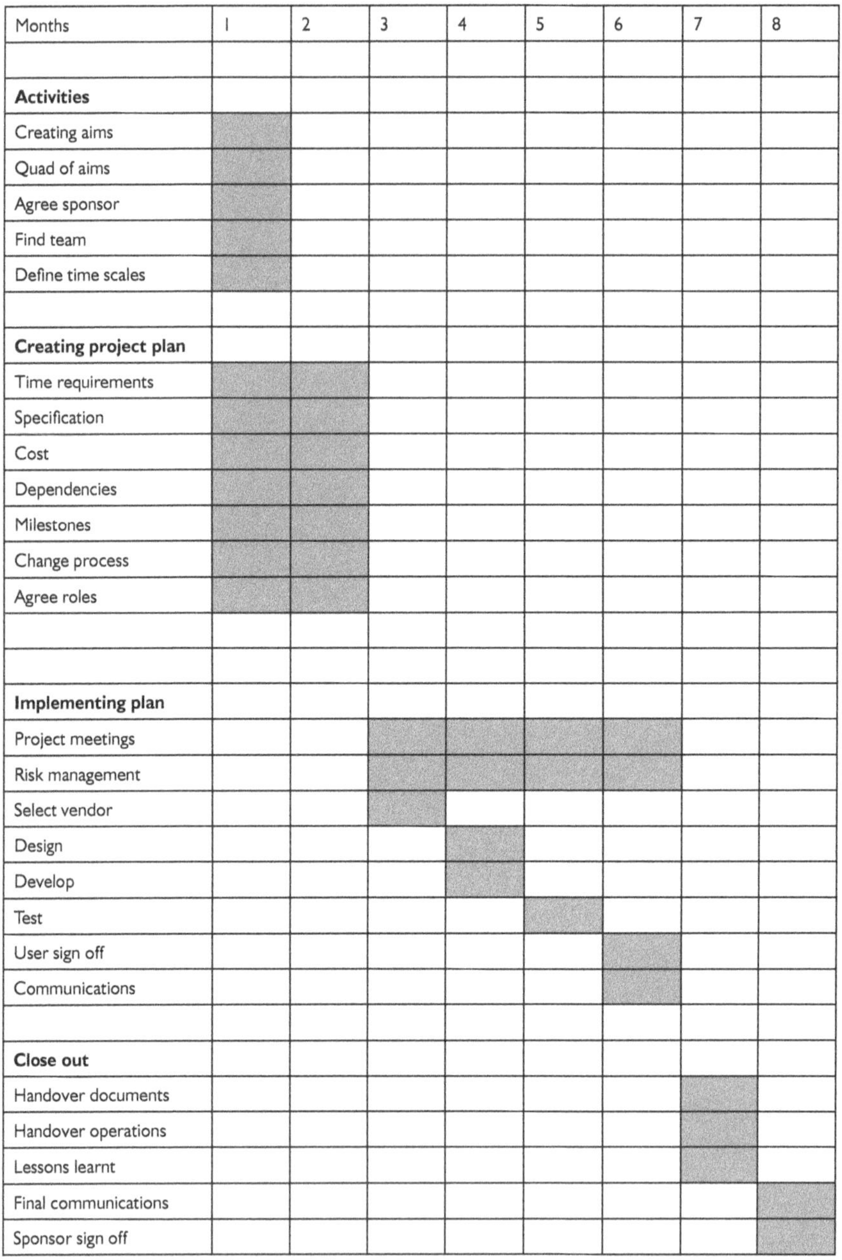

Months	1	2	3	4	5	6	7	8
Activities								
Creating aims	▓							
Quad of aims	▓							
Agree sponsor	▓							
Find team	▓							
Define time scales	▓							
Creating project plan								
Time requirements	▓	▓						
Specification	▓	▓						
Cost	▓	▓						
Dependencies	▓	▓						
Milestones	▓	▓						
Change process	▓	▓						
Agree roles	▓	▓						
Implementing plan								
Project meetings			▓	▓	▓	▓		
Risk management			▓	▓	▓	▓		
Select vendor			▓					
Design				▓				
Develop				▓				
Test					▓			
User sign off						▓		
Communications						▓		
Close out								
Handover documents							▓	
Handover operations							▓	
Lessons learnt							▓	
Final communications								▓
Sponsor sign off								▓

Figure 6.8 Gantt chart

Table 6.6 Project meeting agenda

Project meeting agenda	Actioned
Review of the previous minutes and actions	
Review of progress and status against the outputs of: • time • cost • specification	
Identification and management of key dependencies and constraints	
Notification of risks and issues, including the transfer, mitigation, allocation or acceptance of identified risks within the project	
Review of specific detailed issues	
Agreement of all actions	
Agreement of communication needed with all stakeholders outside the project team	

Monitoring the plan

The implementation and monitoring of plans is the role of the project manager who will be required to manage project teams, communicate with the stakeholders and oversee the delivery of the plans. The project manager may be a dedicated employee seconded or given over to this activity for a time, an employee hired on a part-time basis, or an external contractor hired to provide the support necessary.

A project manager is accountable for the overall delivery of the project. In practice the management of internal project meetings and effective stakeholder communication achieves this.

A typical project meeting will cover the matters listed in Table 6.6.

Communication to stakeholders could involve:

- distributing minutes of the meetings;
- attending one or more of their team meetings to present a project update;
- personal one-to-one meetings to provide opportunities for discussion;
- internal web utilization;
- e-mails;
- phone contact as required.

Closing out the project

The act of formally ending or 'closing out' a project ensures that:

- Delivery as per the quad of aims and project plan has been achieved.
- The hand over from the project team to the day-to-day operations staff is carried out as agreed.

- The sponsor is satisfied with the project outcomes.
- 'Lessons learned' are documented so that the team and others can reflect on successes and avoid any problems that the team has encountered in the future.

The importance of this phase of a project cannot be underestimated. Where it is poorly managed it can lead to particular problems for the organization.

Problems arising as a result of poor project closure include:

- The project manager moves on to a new project before the system installed is tested or bedded down, so issues and remaining risks cannot be properly resolved.
- Project resources including staff are withdrawn before completion, so that not all activities can be satisfactorily completed.
- System bugs remain in the live system with fixes being inadequately installed.
- Poor handover of knowledge from the project team with regard to day-to-day operations so that day-to-day staff finds the output difficult to use.
- Poor documentation and work instructions at the hand-back stage so nothing to refer to after project team has gone.

In summary, projects will likely be a feature of business partner activities. Progressive core competences for an effective business partner should include:

- the knowledge of good practices and being part of a project team;
- the skill of leading a project team;
- the competence of leading multiple projects simultaneously.

CHANGE

Change has two features that can be attributed to it, these are an emotional content and a logical context. We will now examine these two features in relation to resistance to change and enablers of change. Two examples follow of how the logical context can be applied using business process engineering or using six-sigma methods.

Types of resistance to change

When faced with changes the stakeholder groups can be predicted to go through several stages, and they may exhibit typical emotional responses.

The Fisher personal transition model (2012) classifies various stages based on different emotions people are believed to experience during a change process.

Table 6.7 lists the stages and the emotions that would be anticipated during a change process (Adams *et al.*, 1976).

Table 6.7 Emotional responses to change

Stage	Typical emotional response
1. Shock	I am looking for another position, I don't like this.
2. Denial	Change, what change? I will carry on as usual.
3. Awareness	I can see what they are trying to do, but what's in it for me?
4. Acceptance	I can see how I fit into this change and I will do what is required of me. I will just get on with it.
5. Experimentation	I think I will try this out in the new process.
6. Search	I have found different ways of doing things that I could not do before.
7. Integration	I have found the best way of doing things and I am comfortable and confident with what I need to do.

The model suggests that the perceived personal competence levels of staff will fluctuate as they move through the emotional stages, and conventional expectations are that it takes about 18 months for an individual to pass through all the stages and work at a competent level. The business partner needs to be cognizant that change will take time to meet delivery requirements. The broad level of change stages is compounded by the fact that individuals will move at different speeds and there will be a variety of individual resistance issues that may need addressing.

Strategies in dealing with change at an individual level

Resistance to change is the action, or lack of action, taken by individuals when they perceive that a change that is planned or occurring is a threat to them. The change need not be either real or large for resistance to occur. However, when changes are perceived as a threat then resistance will take place. Resistance may take many forms, including active or non- engagement, overt or covert, individual or organized, aggressive or passive stances toward the change.

There are many reasons why individuals resist change. The significant issue to address within a change program is that each individual will have differing reasons to resist or accept the change. The assembly of these individual concerns may then become significant. There will be an element of both logical and emotional reasons to resist or accept change.

In Figure 6.9 individual examples of the causes for resistance to change have been grouped for the purpose of examining potential strategies that can be applied. This model has been developed and applied by the author.

Effective communications strategy

Effective communication strategies should apply in all instances of change.

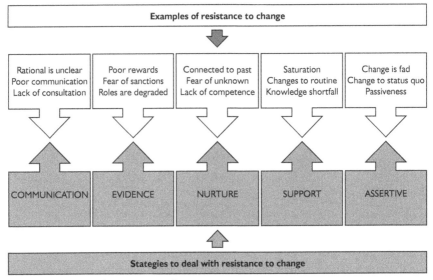

Figure 6.9 Causes of resistance to change

There are many media through which effective communication approaches can take place. They include the existing and established processes of one-to-one personal meetings, objective setting, team meetings, and team briefings.

Effective communication will support these resistance issues:

- *Unclear rationale*: resistance will occur when the rationale for the change is unclear and this is where misconceptions, rumours, concerns and fears are manifested. This can be compounded by poor communication and a lack of consultation with key stakeholders.
- *Poor communication*: this may occur due to poor planning or targeting of the changes, competing requirements and differing priorities.
- *Lack of consultation*: this occurs when there is a need to engage with individuals at a deeper level than just communication. A 'sell' approach will become more acceptable than a 'tell' approach.

Evidential strategy

An evidential strategy is best applied when there are attributes of 'what is in it for me?' traits being exhibited. These expectations from the individual may be both positive and negative. This can have both financial and non- financial elements and may vary significantly between individuals. To mitigate the level of potential resistance to change, the following should be applied:

- clarity
- confidentiality
- fairness

- impartiality
- rationality.

1 *Rewards:* individuals will be motivated and engaged more when it can be demonstrated that the effort is worth it for them personally.
2 *Sanctions:* the fear of sanctions may seem as a threat, for example pay for performance, bonuses and future promotions or employment with the organization.
3 *Roles are degraded:* where the current roles are reduced in status as a result of change and this is likely to impact pride and status within the organization.

Nurturing strategies

Nurturing strategies are best applied when individuals want to change but have difficulty or do not know how too. Approaches should include: extra training, coaching, mentoring, patience and tolerance. That will help to mitigate these types of resistance:

- *Connection to the past*: this will be an emotional element by the individual who may have invested a personal commitment to what is in place. The current old way once was new, and the individual may have been instrumental in its implementation.
- *Fear of the unknown:* this is a common reason for resistance is the fear of perceived threats of the unknown – depending on personality types, the opportunity of improvements needs to be greater than remaining with the status quo.
- *Lack of competence:* this may have been identified as part of the training process – a shortfall of skills to make the transition will be of concern to the individual.

Supportive strategies

Supportive strategies are best utilized when individuals want to change, however they feel constrained in doing so. Supportive strategies include the review of constraining factors, setting of priorities and collaborating with potential solutions that support the individual. The resistance types that this approach will support include:

- *Exhaustion/saturation of the individual*: examples of this include too many initiatives in place, excessive workloads, specific expert skills are in short supply, engaging with the change, dealing with current workloads and legacy issues being created.
- *Changes to routines:* existing known routines are comfort zones for individuals, they know where they stand and they make them secure, so there may be resistance if they do not know what the new routines might be.

- *Concern over knowledge*: individuals may believe the change will mean they have a shortfall in knowledge or expertise to perform the activities.

Assertive strategies

Assertive strategies can be applied where it is recognized that motivation is low and there may be a level of cynicism and resistance. The strategy approach should be to resolve this with an individual basis through one-to-one meetings, objective setting, and if required performance management. A logical and assertive approach will help engage with the emotional content and with the individuals concerned.

When an individual believes that the change activity is a temporary trend and is unlikely to succeed or be completed successfully, there will be little buy in and support for the change. These beliefs are likely to have an emotional content based on past experiences and are evidenced through a person now exhibiting low levels of trust.

- *Change in the status quo*. Opposition can also start from beliefs or observations of the change that individuals hold. For example, individuals who believe that they will not benefit from the change will be doubtful to provide their support, and the opposite will be likely to apply.
- *Passive resistance*. This profile occurs in individuals who are overpowered by unremitting change resigning them selves to it without active engagement. Although they will provide a minimum engagement they will not be openly hostile to the change.

In summary there are a variety of causes that generate the resistance to change. These will have elements of emotional and logical reasons which will need to be addressed. Applying the most effective strategy will support the mitigation or potential elimination of resistance. Dealing with resistance is in effect reacting to and resolving different degrees of potential negativity. The business partner needs to deal with this resistance appropriately as it arises. A more positive and proactive approach is to engage with progressive enablement of change and this now follows.

The enablers to change

To enable change to have positive outcomes there are several key questions that need to be considered:

- How do I manage expectations for the change?
- How quickly will change be adopted?
- What are the key attributes and elements for successful change?
- What is the scale of change and which methods should be considered?
- What is the previous experience of this organizational change?

A review of these questions now follows with examples of the models that can be applied.

Managing expectations for change?

My own model relates to managing expectations. Managing the expectations of the individuals and the stakeholders who will be impacted is a critical part of managing change. Mismanaging the expectations of stakeholders can lead to:

- anger
- complaints
- frustration
- loss of confidence
- trying to go back to old ways and legacy systems/processes
- sabotage in extreme cases
- litigation.

The initial expectation is that once change occurs there is an immediate improvement, but this rarely occurs. In fact, my own model describes six stages in managing stakeholder expectations. Communication to stakeholders that the initial change will likely cause deterioration in the short term is also key to managing the long-term expectations of change. Table 6.8 lists the six stages of the model.

Some examples of barriers to the move from stage 1 to stage 5 are:

- lack of training;
- those impacted not attending training and education sessions;
- keeping to old methods, despite a new method being in place;
- over-reliance on an extended parallel run of processes or systems, and then users failing to switch over;
- resistance and reluctance to change.

Table 6.8 The six stages of the model

	Stage	Anticipated expectation
1	Commencement stage	This is what we do now
2	Installation stage	The service is inferior and is not what is expected
3	Bedding down stage	The service is what is expected but it is inferior, as I still do not know how to use this
4	Assimilation stage	The service is superior but expectation on the change neutral
5	Efficiency stage	This is much better, I can see the benefits to me
6	Effectiveness stage	This is what we do now (the new 1)

The first five stages are illustrated in Figure 6.10.

The sixth stage is when the change has been fully embedded. The new 'to-be' model becomes the existing 'as-is' model. Stage 5 becomes Stage 6 when efficiency of the change moves into the delivery of effective outcomes (Figure 6.11).

Managing expectations can be key to ensuring that powerful stakeholders support the change through critical stages. Moving directly from stage 1 directly to stage 6 is unlikely to occur.

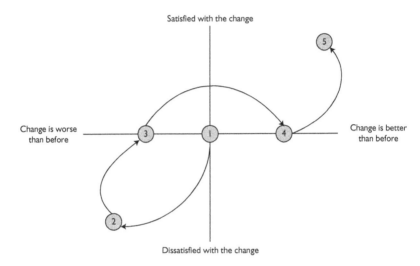

Figure 6.10 The first five stages of the model

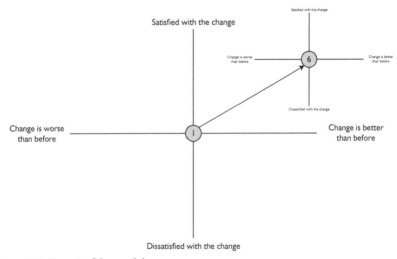

Figure 6.11 Stage 6 of the model

Table 6.9 Rogers' adoption categories

Innovators	Enthusiastic about anything new
	Quick to adopt and adapt to any new changes
	Thrive on change and become bored with doing the same thing over a long period of time
Early adopters	Interested in creating value from something new
	Require just a small amount of persuasion to change
	Are keen to change if they can see the reasons
The majority	Innovators and early adopters will influence this group as change starts
	Keen to improve the effectiveness of new processes relating to change
	Will change when they can assimilate how it works
	Will determine whether an innovative practice is embedded
	Need a different support structure from early adopters with more emphasis on teaching practice and more stability
Laggards	Sceptics opposed to anything new
	Resist any new changes and find it difficult to adopt new ways of doing things
	See change as a threat and not an opportunity

How quickly will change be adopted?

Rogers' adoption curve (2003) is a model devised to explain how ideas and technology spread within a population by considering their speed and level of adoption by different groups. The model can also be applied to non-technology changes. He categorizes five groups within a population where some groups will be more receptive to change than others. Table 6.9 shows each group's different features. Their speed of adoption is represented diagrammatically in Figure 6.12. The typical profile of accepting and adoption in percentages is shown in Table 6.10.

A business partner involved in change needs to be cognizant of the speed of acceptance. Focusing initially upon the innovators and early adopters, these groups will, in effect influence, and drag the rest along through peer pressure – the early and late majority, then finally the laggards.

What are the key attributes and elements for change?

The ADKAR method (Hiatt 2006) is a result-orientated management tool; it can be used to diagnose the root causes for resistances, barrier points to changes and also a focus on effective communication. Table 6.11 shows the model in the context of business partnering.

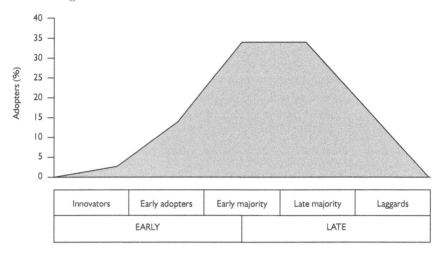

Figure 6.12 Rogers' adoption curve

Table 6.10 Rogers' adoption profiles

Adoption profiles	Typical percentage within a population facing change
Those who like innovating	3%
Employees who adopt very quickly	15%
The majority of employees	36%
Employees who adopt more slowly	35%
Those who do not wish to change i.e. laggards	11%

Business process engineering

Process analysis of the service content

One of the basic requirements for the business partner is to appreciate how the stakeholder's processes or service requirements work. Without engaging upon the stakeholder's processes, there will be knowledge gaps of what changes could be targeted and this may impede the support and expert advice from the business partner. Process mapping and then analysis is a method aimed at fostering a positive culture to examine and improve end-to-end processes in support of stakeholder targets (Swientozielskyj 2014).

The aim of process analysis and mapping is to:

* determine what needs changing;
* target where the business partner should review, analyse and, if necessary, intervene;
* achieve performance improvement;

Table 6.11 ADKAR model

	Enablers of change	Examples of the enablers that the business partner can apply to support change
A	*Awareness* of the need of change	• Dealing with rumours and any miscommunication • Reviewing the receptiveness of those being impacted is it positive/negative or neutral • Early engagement based on the power and influence matrix (see Chapter 3) • Positive, credible and clear communication
D	*Desire* to support and participate in the change	• Developing a positive future state e.g. the 'to-be' position • Engaging those being impacted by collaborative workshops • Using customer input to developing the final solution • Identifying early adopters who will develop a sense of affiliation and support to the change
K	*Knowledge* of how to change	• Reviewing what documentation or procedures might need updating after the change • Developing detailed training programmes for those who will be directly impacted by the change • Educating the managers of those being trained of what and why training is taking place • Informing senior stakeholders
A	*Ability* to implement the required skills and behaviours	• User testing and training • Competence based assessments • Final user-sign off • Use mentoring and coaching
R	*Reinforcement* to sustain the change	• Celebrate success • Personal recognition • Incentive systems • Compensation changes

• identify high and low value-added processes to enhance or eliminate them;
• target where and what gets performance measured;
• enable continuous improvement and support excellence;
• integrate processes across functions.

A business partner can either engage reactively in having to deal with problems that occur, or proactively to create added value solutions. Process mapping is a method of identifying and understanding the sequence of steps required by an activity to deliver outputs or outcomes. This can be either used proactively or reactively. Once a process has been defined it can be measured and then improved. Inputs flow into a process, are worked on and outputs

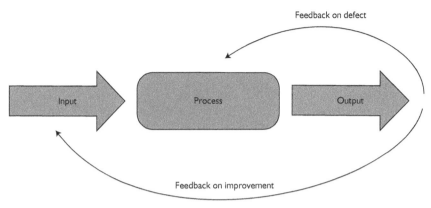

Figure 6.13 Process map

are produced. Feedback loops identify and remedy any defects in the output or exploit any improvements. Inputs, either manually generated or emanating from an information system, activate a process. These may be the outputs from a previous process. The business partner may need to support the stakeholder to focus on the added value of the whole system. Organizational difficulties with certain processes may require rapid performance improvements for the stakeholders.

The basic process model is shown in Figure 6.13 in a process map that shows the flow of the events from the start to the finish of a process (end-to-end).

Inputs

The start and end of a process can have cross-functional boundaries and be difficult for the business partner to identify. One of the challenges for the business partner is to identify and clarify and where necessary, alter the boundaries of the responsibility and accountability for the end-to-end process (Figure 6.14).

Process

This is the sequence of activities that transforms various inputs towards delivered outputs. The business partner should analyse the contribution of each activity in the process and then evaluate it by analysing what actually occurs and why. Consideration should be given to who performs the activity and the method they use, as well as how it is controlled. The RACI model will support this analysis.

Determining which processes should be investigated requires considering the cost of a process and the performance outputs or outcomes levels it achieves.

The added value of carrying out the process helps to establish whether the process should take place or be eliminated or rationalized.

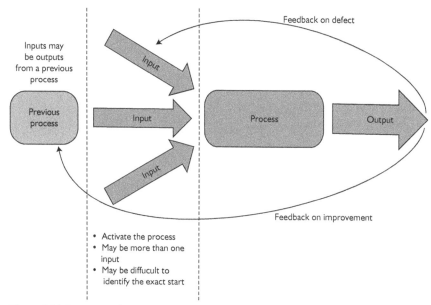

Figure 6.14 Inputs to a business process

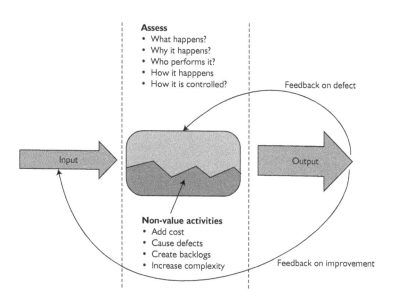

Figure 6.15 Process

It is important for the business partner who is analysing a process to distinguish between value and non-value added activities.

Added value processes significantly improve an organization's ability to:

- improve customer service to the stakeholder;
- maintain compliance standards that are their functional specialism;
- reduce cost;
- speed up cycle times and service delivery.

Superior performance in a process will improve efficiency and effectiveness and will be a source of competitive advantage. This is what the business partner should target.

Processes which do not add value have a limited impact or restrict the ability of an organization to deliver its outputs, outcomes, or objectives. They are likely to increase costs, create unnecessary complexity, and result in backlogs or defects.

No organization intentionally creates activities which do not add value within their processes, but they can arise as a result of:

- changes to inputs or methods;
- failure to address defects;
- informal workarounds being adopted as a temporary fix (outside the formal system/rules);
- poorly trained or under-resourced staff;
- failure to benchmark performance;
- poor design, documentation and understanding of the process.

Outputs

Outputs are the end result of the process. For example, to analyse product sales there are three potential outputs:

- new customers (the desirable outputs);
- existing customers kept (the minimum required output);
- existing customers lost (a defect or error).

Assessment of the outputs from a process will require evaluating not just whether the output has been generated, but whether it has gone to the right person in the right department, in the correct format, on time and without errors. Issues such as quality and customer service are as important as cost and compliance (Figure 6.16).

Feedback loops

A feedback loop is there to inform an input or process that it:

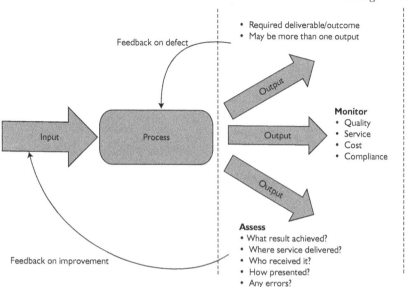

Figure 6.16 Outputs of a business process

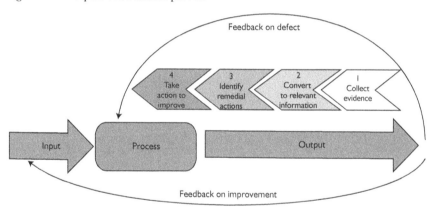

Figure 6.17 Feedback loop

- has worked
- has not worked
- can be improved.

Feedback loops ensure that standards are maintained and objectives are met. Where results are unacceptable, they allow for the business partner to diagnose the problem and the immediate corrections as well as longer-term implementation of improvements and solutions.

In the simple model in Figure 6.17, the feedback loop will either require action within the process or the input to the process.

A feedback loop involves four distinct stages:

1 *Evidence:* process outputs should be measured, captured, and stored – this will come from data being received.
2 *Relevance:* the feedback should be communicated to the person responsible, not in the initial form in which it was received, but within a framework that makes it understandable. Without direct relevance to the individual information or data, it is unusable.
3 *Consequence:* the analysis should identify several options that can be applied.
4 *Action:* The individual will have choices in their behaviours, choices and actions they take. The individual will need to be encouraged that improvements will continually need to be made to the standard required.

Methods of improvement

The business partner should have an in-depth understanding of the processes or service which they support. They should either be in a position to deploy these directly or commission and then manage third parties to deliver the improvements required. There are several techniques that the business partner may deploy in improving the overall business processes they support and serve. In addition organizational difficulties with certain processes may require rapid performance improvements. These include:

Evaluating leading indicators

This type of indicator signals future events. For example, an amber traffic light indicates the coming of the red light. Interest rates are thought to be a good leading indicator for stock market falls and traders may anticipate and speculate upon the trends in the economy, even though they are not always correct.

Analysing lagging indicators

A lagging indicator is one that trails an event. For example, the red and amber traffic lights are a lagging indicator for the red light. The use of a lagging indicator confirms what has occurred in the past. Continually monitoring these as a trend they may identify actions that might require attention. For example, a trend that costs are increasing might need attention. A second example, unemployment is a well recognised lagging indicator. If the unemployment rate is rising, it indicates that the economy has been doing poorly. Lagging indicators have the features of being difficult to influence, output-based and are more easily measured. Leading indicators have the features of being more easily influenced, input-based, but more difficult to measure.

Utilizing benchmarking methods

Benchmarking is the technique of contrasting organizational inputs, processes, outcomes and performance metrics to other comparable standards. These may include either internal comparisons within the organization or external standards. Benchmarking will review the efficiency (doing it the right way) and effectiveness (doing the right thing).

Business process re-engineering (BPR)

In business process re-enginerring, a process is reviewed end-to-end from first principles to eradicate any activities that do not add value.

Balanced scorecard

If there is a balanced scorecard in place this may also act a leading indicator for intervention.

Deployment of the 4C model

The 4C model is discussed in Chapter 5.

Six sigma and lean tools

The prime focus for the six sigma method is to reduce defects. To achieve six sigma the organization must not have more than 3.4 defects per million of product manufacturing, processes, or service delivery. This focus will review what changes are required to support better outcomes for stakeholders. The continuous focus to achieve stable and predictable results will drive changes to achieve exceptional or world-class outcomes.

What is six sigma?

Organisational activities have five characteristics that define the end-to-end activities from the end user, customer or stakeholder perspectives. These support the definition of standards, expectations, or targets that are being sought. These are:

- measuring critical aspects of the end-to-end activities that requires to be improved – this will be as a result of the collection of the accurate information of how activities work;
- analysing the information and process maps to review and check interactive interactions;
- improving the current activities based on systematic analysis using a variety of techniques;

- controlling the required or planned deviations standards that are set. Ideally, the interventions will be proactive and will correct defects before they actually occur.

The stakeholder will require resolute leadership and engagement from their business partners and their teams. The approach will be statistical and evidential as opposed to verbal or anecdotal observations.

Key defined roles for six sigma

Six sigma uses terms from the martial arts world to describe the importance and levels of roles. A martial arts practitioner black belt would be recognized as someone more skilled than a green or yellow belt and a master black belt more senior still.

The key roles and responsibilities are defined and explained below.

Executives will:

- create the vision for change;
- create a culture within the organization that will promote the use of leading methodology and tools;
- define the strategic goals and measures of the organization;
- establish the required targets;
- make resources available.

The senior deployment champion (six sigma) will:

- act as a liaison between the executives and deployment champions;
- design the support systems;
- ensure effective communications;
- define the outcomes required;
- review the priorities;
- report to stakeholders on progress;
- develop and deliver the training required;
- remove barriers for the team activities;
- select and support the project champions.

The project champion (role could be merged with that of the senior deployment champion on simpler projects) will:

- align the resources that are required;
- communicate the progress of projects to the deployment champion and process owners;
- lead upon project identification, prioritization, and defining the project scope;
- select and mentor the 'black belts'.

The 'master black belt' will:

- mentor 'black belts' and 'green belts';
- become an expert in six sigma tools and concepts;
- train 'black belts' and ensure they are properly applying the methodology and tools;
- maintain the training material, document standards and compile updates;
- work on high-level projects across stakeholder groups.

'Black belt' (role could be merged with 'master black belt' on simpler projects) will:

- be responsible for leading, executing, and completing projects;
- report progress according to the project definition and scope;
- support the identification of project opportunities and scope;
- transfer knowledge to other 'black belts' and the organization;
- teach and mentor team members in the six sigma methodology and tools.

The 'green belt' will:

- be an effective team member within a black belt team or the process owner;
- be trained in a subset of the six sigma methodology and tools;
- work on small scope projects, typically in his/her respective work areas.

The process owner, will:

- be an active team member;
- be responsible for maintaining the project's gains;
- act to remove barriers to the changes that are required;
- take ownership of the process changes when it is completed;

These roles and responsibilities have been explained in relation to using a six-sigma approach. Many of these can be deployed in relation to projects in general.

Summary for six sigma

Six sigma are business methods that enable organizations to:

- improve change outcomes;
- achieve high levels of customer satisfaction;
- install a culture of continuous improvements;
- meet world-class quality standards;
- drive towards almost zero defects.

Chapter summary

Change is to progress from an old 'as-is' state towards a new 'to-be' state. This chapter outlined the scope and type of change. It provided a 'line of sight' to examples of change approaches that can be applied. What causes and drives changes, what resistance might be expected and how to overcome them have been reviewed. More positively, the enablers of positive and successful change have been defined and explored with the relevant methodologies that can be applied. Change is powered by strategic, tactical and operational causes; these impact the attainment of goals, aims, targets, outcomes, outputs and objectives. Applying the optimum change model will enable enhanced successes and mitigate the risks of failure. Change has emotional and logical features and change is a constant for successful organizations. The final stage of the general model is the outcome stage which is explored in Chapter 7.

References

Adams, J., Hayes, J., and Hopson, B. (1976) *Transition, Understanding and Managing Personal Change.* London: Wiley-Blackwell.

CGMA (2013a) *Essential Tools for Management Accountants.* London: CGMA.

CGMA (2013b) 'From insight to impact unlocking opportunities in big data'. Retrieved 8 March 2015 from http://www.cgma.org/Resources/Reports/DownloadableDocuments/From_insight_to_impact-unlocking_the_opportunities_in_big_data

Fisher, J. (2012) 'The personal transition curve'. Retrieved 16 June 2015 from http://www.businessballs.com/freepdfmaterials/fisher-transition-curve-2012bb.pdf

Greiner, L. (1972) 'Evolution and revolution as organizations grow'. Retrieved 14 November 2015 from http://www.ils.unc.edu/daniel/131/cco4/Greiner

Hiatt, Jeffrey (2006) *ADKAR: A Model for Change in Business, Government and Our Community.* Fort Collins, CO: Prosci Learning Center Publications.

IMF (2000) 'Globalization: threat or opportunity'. Retrieved 14 November 2015 from https://www.imf.org/external/np/exr/ib/2000/041200to.htm#II

Rogers, E.M. (2003) *Diffusion of Innovations*, 5th edn. New York: Simon & Schuster International.

Swientozielskyj, S. (2014) *Certificate in Shared Services.* London: Chartered Institute of Management Accountants.

Wikipedia (n.d.) 'Big data'. Retrieved 8 March 2015 from http://en.wikipedia.org/wiki/Big_data

7 The outcomes stage

Outcomes that occur are a result of the quality of inputs, effort, and resources invested to achieve them.

> Insanity is doing the same thing in the same way and expecting a different outcome.
>
> Old Chinese proverb

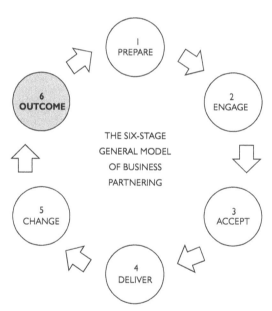

Figure 7.1 Outcomes overview

This chapter examines the organizational, personal outcomes, and the essential requirements of a business-partnering program.

Knowledge components considered in this chapter

Organizational outcomes

- organizational
- stakeholder
- team.

Personal outcomes

- rewards
- personal development
- the deepening of trust
- the development of ethics.

Essentials of a business-partnering program

- set up
- governance
- lessons learned.

INTRODUCTION

In Chapters 2 to 6 I outlined that the specific outcomes of any operating model will be unique and dependent on many variables. Effective business partnering will enhance the outcomes of the operating model that they support. In this chapter I will specifically focus upon the outcomes of the entity that the business partner operates within and their own personal outcomes (Figure 7.2).

The knowledge, skill, and competences of the business partner will help to deliver, improve, or influence changes to the requirements of the operating model. The broad outcomes of this will be; entity outcomes for the organization as a whole, the business stakeholders they support, and the teams they engage with. In addition, there will be personal outcomes for the business partner including rewards, personal development, the deepening of trust and development of an ethical approach. The review of both the entity and personal business partnering outcomes now follow.

The scope of entity outcomes will be reviewed and will include the following groupings:

- organizational (change)
- stakeholders (improve)
- stakeholder teams (deliver).

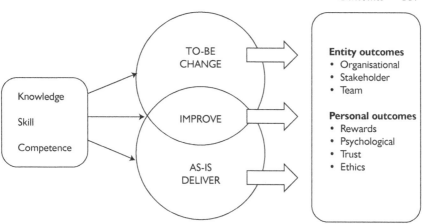

Figure 7.2   Knowledge, skills and competences

Organizational outcomes

The organizational outcomes should be based on mission statement, targets, and the operating values that support it. A mission statement defines what the organization is, and why it exists. The mission statement should include elements of the primary customers, the products or services that are being provided, and the geographical locations that are operated within. The values link to the mission statement and are the principles that guide the organizations internal and external relationships. An effective organization will link the strategic outcomes for the organization through to its mission statement.

Each organization will have a unique mission statement and operating principles that support it. It is what differentiates organizations within the markets or sectors that they operate in. As a direct consequence the organizational outcomes will be different. It is important that the business partners are aware of their own organizational circumstances and the part that they influence. An outcome method that can be applied to organizations is illustrated in Figure 7.3.

An important framework from outcome theories is Duignan's outcomes system. Figure 7.3 relates to this theory, which can be applied to organizational outcomes that the business partner and their stakeholders will support.

The three drivers to the outcomes that relate to the organizations' mission statement and operating values are planning, monitoring, and evaluating. These impact and influence seven factors, which are reviewed below:

1 *Line of sight:* how the organizational outcomes directly relate to the business partner and stakeholders. This occurs when the aims, goals, targets,

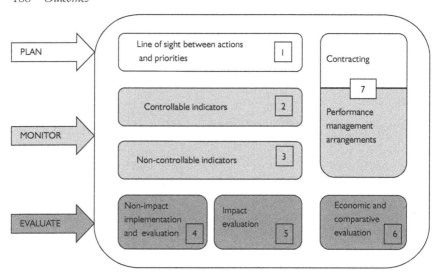

Figure 7.3 Organizational outcomes

outcomes, outputs, and objectives are all aligned towards and clearly linked to the delivery of the organizations mission statement.

2 *Controllable indicators*: these are measures of some of the outcomes that are required. Controllable indicators have the features that their measurement can be evidenced. Examples will include organizational project, activity, or direct interventions.

3 *Non-controllable indicators* are indicators that are impacted by influences that cannot be directly controlled by the individual or the organization, for example, market share.

4 *Non-impact evaluation*: while controllable and non-controllable indicators are analysed or reviewed regularly, this type of evaluation concentrates on enhancing detailed or one off evaluations.

5 *Impact evaluation* is the direct relationship to what has instigated the outcomes to occur (i.e. did the intervention make the intended impact).

6 *Comparative and economic evaluation* contrasts dissimilar impacts and evaluates their advantages and financial effects. In this way, different impacts can provide insights that can then be contrasted. An example of this would be the payback on an investment on two completely unique and different projects.

7 *Contracting, accountability, and performance management* agreements will relate to the value chains that stakeholders and business partners operate within. This will also include outside stakeholders such as suppliers and customers.

Although the specific outcomes for organizations may be unique to them, the use of the model above may support:

- a new business partner seeking an understanding of how the organization drives outcomes towards fulfilling the mission statement;
- an existing business partner and their stakeholder seeking and creating additional enterprise value;
- the enhancement of understanding of how the stakeholder, their teams and business partner can improve their alignment to the requirements of the organizational outcomes;
- the organizational measurement systems of the balanced scorecard and KPIs provide an insight to activities that need monitoring or delivering;
- fundamental major changes are not measured or identified but this may be required.

A review of the stakeholder outcomes now follows.

Stakeholder outcomes

The stakeholder outcomes are likely to be a balance between:

- managing the short-term delivery requirements within their current 'as-is' position that they operate within;
- improving the medium term delivery with their teams;
- supporting the longer-term aims towards the future 'to-be' organization.

Both the delivery and change stages may be the precursor to outcomes being delivered.

Delivery has been reviewed in Chapter 5 and this has included a review of business, delivery, and operating models, type and definitions of delivery, and the constraints and enablers for delivery. The delivery support methods were reviewed and these included; SWOT, risk management, 4C model, KPIs, budgets, and also functional methods of delivering outputs.

Change was covered in Chapter 6 and this included organizational perspectives in relation to what causes and drives change, the causes of the resistance to change and, finally, change enablers. The specific methods, which were considered included benchmarking, technology implementations, business process engineering, six sigma, project management, and balanced scorecards.

The stakeholder's drive for efficiency and effectiveness improvements to enhance outcomes can be aided by the application of a variety of models and methods. The model that will be reviewed within this context of driving outcomes will be Kotter's (1996) model. Although the model is generally applied to organizational change, the end point is to have sustainable outcomes. The stakeholder supported by their business partner can adopt the principles to drive improved outcomes within their own accountabilities and responsibilities. This will create the right climate for outcomes by engaging and enabling them and finally sustaining them.

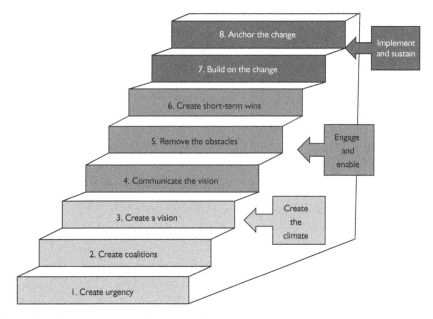

Figure 7.4 The eight steps in Kotter's model

There are eight steps to drive the organizational outcomes (Figure 7.4). The steps to be taken, in relation to Kotter's model, are now explained.

Step 1: Create urgency

This is reinforced if the organization supports or is requiring improvements to take place. The development of a sense of urgency around the need for improvement will be a catalyst for the initial motivation by the stakeholder.

Step 2: Form a powerful coalition

This takes effective management and noticeable backing from important personnel within an organization. Although the leadership will come from the key stakeholder, the business partners can align themselves to being a key competent expert and team member. They will operate as a virtual team, persistently pushing and communicating the outcomes being sought.

Step 3: Create a vision

A clear vision can support everyone's understanding of what and why the improvements are required. Linking new ideas and potential solutions to a vision that all impacted employees can positively engage with and relate to will motivate them.

Step 4: Communicate the vision

This will include:

- it is important to 'walk the talk': actions are key;
- being consistent with the behaviours that are to be expected;
- embedding it into all activities, such as solving problems and decision making;
- frequent and powerful messaging;

Step 5: Remove obstacles

This will include:

- identifying individuals whom oppose the initiative being implemented;
- reviewing activities or procedures that are creating obstacles;
- continually checking for barriers;
- empowering employees to execute the vision, to help the improvements move forward.

Step 6: Create short-term wins

This will include:

- developing short-term achievable outputs that can deliver;
- an initial focus on short-term success;
- celebrating the early successes within the team;
- communicating the successes outside the team.

Step 7: Build on the change

This should consider:

- not claiming overall success too early;
- embedding the change by rewards;
- consistent and constant messaging;
- alignment of personal objectives.

Step 8: Anchor the improvements made

Finally, to make any improvements embedded, they should become part of the core of the activities that are taking place. Corporate behaviours and attitudes influence what is prioritized, so the thinking behind the initial vision, needs cascading and embedding into daily activities. It is also important that the organization's executives persist in backing the transformation. This should included new employees joining the organization. If visible, enduring, and engagement of key stakeholders is lost then this will be detrimental to the delivery of potential outcomes.

The business partner will be unlikely to be directly accountable for the delivery of targeted improvements, however they can be a key resource to support the stakeholder outcomes. The specifics of how the team outcomes relate now follow.

Team outcomes

The business partner in supporting the team outcomes may perform different roles ranging from leading activities or participating in the team outcome requirements. Regardless of the role performed within the team, there will be a continuous requirement for conflict resolution. Dealing with conflict at a task or a personal level will need resolution before outputs can be efficiently delivered. The team learning outcomes will be a comprehensive understanding of 'what' needs delivering, be it aims, goals, targets, outcomes, outputs or objectives and 'how' it is to be delivered through social cohesion and learning how to operate as an effective team. This is illustrated in Figure 7.5.

The assessment of how effective a team is can be supported from research and theories. According to Hackman, team effectiveness can be defined in terms of three criteria:

1 *Outputs*: the final outputs produced by the team must meet or exceed the standards set by key constituents within the organization. This defines what is to be delivered.
2 *Social processes*: the internal social processes operating as the team interacts should enhance, or at least maintain, the group's ability to work together in the future. This defines how it is to be delivered.
3 *Learning*: the experience of working in the team environment should act to satisfy rather than aggravate the personal needs of team members.

(Hackman, 1987)

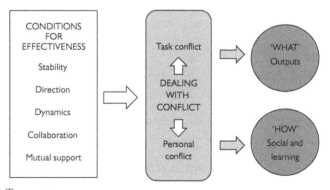

Figure 7.5 Team outcomes

This supports the assimilation of what and how learning circumstances can be more effectively applied in the future.

These attributes of the team tasks and activity performance criteria support the group outcome processes.

Team conflict is a basic part of any team. The main qualities that support effective teams are:

- the culture of the team;
- balancing priorities on an agreed basis;
- accommodating behaviours to each other;
- team mutual helpfulness;
- the resolution of conflicts in a positive manner.

Team unity is considered as a universal basic of all great teams. Unity enables better co-operation, self-fulfilment and group relationships. These features will support the team's confidence in each other when faced with barriers, problems or challenges that need resolution. According to Hackman:

> There are also five conditions that research has shown to optimize the effectiveness of the team:
> 1 *Real team:* stability in the group membership over time.
> 2 *Compelling direction*: a clear purpose that relies on end goals.
> 3 *Enabling structure:* the group's dynamic must be performing successfully and not poorly.
> 4 *Social support*: the group must have a system to collaborate properly
> 5 *Coaching:* opportunities for coaching to provide additional support and help.
>
> (Hackman, 2002)

In summary, the outcomes for an effective team are to know what to do and how to do it within a repeatable method or system. When the system is successful then all team members will be satisfied, have emotional commitment to the team, have pride in their performance, and support the task commitments to each other. This will result in the effective delivery of outcomes.

Beyond these initial outcomes there are further positive secondary impacts. First, if the effective team system and performance can be continued to be delivered, the outcomes will continue to improve, and where possible can be benchmarked to world-class standards (CGMA, 2012)

This is when the team moves beyond delivering at the as–is stage, they move to improvement and finally change to a new enhanced model and standard of performing.

Second, when team members leave a high-performing group they can use their knowledge skills and competences to help support the building of new high-performing teams that deliver exceptional outputs.

This section completes the review around achievement of the organizational or entity outcomes. The review of personal outcomes of rewards, personal development, trust, and ethics now follow.

PERSONAL OUTCOMES

Rewards

The short-term financial reward for the business partner will be evidenced through normal pay increases and, where they apply, bonuses and performance-related pay. What should be more attractive to the business partner in the long term will be promotion to senior roles. It is the non-financial rewards that are likely to drive long-term financial rewards that the business partner may be seeking, and these will include:

- job satisfaction
- job enrichment
- job enlargement
- increased motivation
- leadership development
- personal development
- recognition and appreciation.

Job satisfaction

Organizations cannot directly impact personal job satisfaction, however, they can enable this to occur. The use of professional selection methods will ensure that business partners are selected and placed in positions that are most

Figure 7.6 Non-financial rewards

suited for them. There is a relationship between personal fulfilment and good client provision and support. This link will support positive engagement with stakeholders and their teams.

Research has analysed that when employees reported higher satisfaction with work facilitation and career development, customers reported higher service quality (Schneider & Bowen, 1985). Schneider and Bowen showed how employee attitudes and various human resources practices correlated with higher customer satisfaction measures, thus indicating key levers to improve customer satisfaction. Conversely, the business partner who has been involuntarily placed in a business partner role through an organizational change is unlikely to commence and continue with positive job satisfaction.

Job enrichment

The underlying principle for job enrichment is to increase the opportunity of the business partners position or role with a greater diversity of projects and responsibilities that require self-motivation and provide personal development opportunities. The objective is to provide increased experience of accountabilities and responsibilities that relate to more senior positions, this is where positive engagement with stakeholders would support this requirement.

This is an opportunity for the business partner to utilize their influencing skills to seek higher challenges to deliver. There are both advantages and disadvantages for job enrichment for the business partner and these are shown in Table 7.1.

Table 7.1 Job enrichment

Advantages	Renewal	Reduction in boredom, making new contacts, thinking about new career options, change viewpoint.
	Exploration	Trying new skill, developing new relationships, testing management and administration skills.
	Specialisation	Re-education, in-depth exploration, using specialist skills, meeting needs that were under serviced or supported.
Disadvantages	Balance	Time allocation, tough decisions about workload, time from regular assignments, balancing workloads.
	Clarity	Lack of information needed to be successful, lack of clear plans and goals, guidance on time and priorities.
	Orientation	Lack of structures, not being taught new responsibilities, difficulty in learning new networks, lack of instruction.

Source: Fourman and Jones, 1997

After the early phases of taking a new a position, the business partner is likely to proactively seek job enrichment with a view of balancing the advantages and disadvantages that might apply.

Job enlargement

Job enlargement aims to increase the scope of a business partner's position through extending the range of current accountabilities and responsibilities. Enlargement involves combining various activities in the workplace to a current existing role. This can contradict the principle of business partner specialization where an individual worker performs activities for which the responsibilities are always clear. This can impact negatively if the enlarged position becomes mundane and provides no real challenge or development for the individual. If used to a great degree it can lead to an excessive workload that cannot be managed by the individual. The benefits of job enlargement include: gaining a variety of new skills, improved learning capacity, and widening the range of activities for the business partner.

The business partner is unlikely to proactively seek job enlargement from a personal perspective, unless they are not currently challenged with the role or there are monetary, or other motivational rewards, that might apply.

Increased motivation

The business partner is already likely to have a high level of personal motivation. Supporting and engaging with positive team motivation will boost and enrich personal motivation. Increased motivation will be enhanced through team behaviours, attributes, and norms.

Team behaviours

Examples of motivational positive team behaviours include:

1 *Optimism and enthusiasm:* positive thinking is possibly the most important behaviour of a high-performing team. The 'can do' attitude under a variety of obstacles and challenges will facilitate positive solutions being sought.
2 *Belief in each other:* a high-performing team will believe they can collectively meet commitments and deadlines together. They believe in each other's ability, embrace diversity, and trust one another.
3 *Praise:* most individuals will appreciate genuine praise for a job well done and taking the time to give sincere and genuine thanks in front of their peers will boost their self-esteem. Team members will appreciate that their hard work and achievements have been noticed.
4 *Honesty:* team members are open and honest with each other and will increase motivation and trust. The high-performing team aims to support an atmosphere where employees are comfortable to speak openly without the fear of any recriminations.

Attributes

Examples of motivational team attributes include:

- *Mutual professional support:* in any team there will be elements of failure, difficulty and challenge in meeting outputs and objectives. When things go wrong or not to plan the level of mutual support without any attributable blame is a key observation of a successful team.
- *Personal support:* mutual personal support has the same attributes as professional support. When personal events or circumstances occur outside the work environment, supporting these in a selfless and supportive way will be appreciated. This will enhance the individual's commitment to the team and leader they support.
- *Communications:* the team that spends time communicating with each other will improve personal connections, create new ideas and develop positive solutions. High-performing teams understand that effective communication will 'make or break' the team outputs and degree of objectives being met.

Norms

Examples of motivational team norms include:

- *Continual demonstration of integrity:* a lack of integrity within a team damages morale and cohesiveness very quickly. Being prepared to demonstrate integrity and support team members consistently will enhance a perspective of mutual professional respect.
- *Challenge:* the high-performing team challenges the status quo and works collaboratively to transform the business.
- *Responsibility:* taking individual responsibility is crucial in any team. Individuals will take control when they are confident and realize their efforts influence decisions and outcomes for the success of the whole team.
- *Focus:* a successful team will work in unison to meet common requirements and needs. The high-performing team understands the direction they are taking and they also understand the difficulties ahead.

Business partner motivation will be enriched when the team's motivation is high. A high-performing business partner will proactively and positively support the team behaviours, attitudes and norms. The impact and reward of this will be an increased self-awareness of their own enhanced motivational levels and how they are impacting the team.

Leadership development

The business partner should have an excellent opportunity to develop and demonstrate leadership capabilities; this will be dependent on their own

Table 7.2 Leadership skills

Leadership skill	The business partner opportunities and linkages to develop leadership skills, knowledge and competences
1 Team understanding	• An effectual leader will know his or her own requirements and personality profile; the business partner will have evaluated these • The leader will know and appreciate the personalities and support these individually with the team • Each team member will be treated with respect • There will be a self-assurance and conviction within the team that the outputs will be delivered
2 Resource management	• Resources include all the requirements necessary to deliver the outcome or objective being sought • Resources also include team knowledge, skills and competences being used • The approach incorporates the motivation to achieve outputs and a real committed conviction it can be achieved • The head of the team will use the relevant talents of the group to meet delivery expectations, the team participants gain experience and improve knowledge and skills
3 Communicating	• To enhance the competence of obtaining information and gaining individuals' insights e.g. checking out your understanding of their views • To develop the competence of providing relevant knowledge or insights upon subjects. To internalize what has been said before responding e.g. think before you speak • Support an open dialogue • Check out your understanding of what has been said
4 Planning	• Preparation is an critical organizational activity • Reviewing options and considering the alternatives • Understanding and applying planning methods • Understanding the trade-off between time, quality and cost • Understanding constraints and enablers to the plan
5 Influencing team performance	• Establishing SMART objectives will support common understanding • Developing positive team behaviours, norms and attributes • Understanding team dynamics • Setting professional standards
6 Evaluating	• Assessing what needs to take place supports the evaluation of the outputs required and aligns everyone to them • Suggesting methods that enhance outputs for the team • Understanding risks and opportunitie
7 Setting an example	• Establishing a confident and personable role model for others to emulate • Using professional approaches • Being approachable

Leadership skill	*The business partner opportunities and linkages to develop leadership skills, knowledge and competences*
8 Representing the group	• Positive advocacy of the team • Working under matrix management processes • Exhibiting expert knowledge • Consultative and collaborative engagement with other stakeholders
9 Expertise	• Evaluating processes • Understanding different delivery requirements and how they interrelate with each other • Professional expertise

personal motivation and professional circumstances. Table 7.2 shows nine leadership skills and examples of how a high-performing business partner may demonstrate opportunities or linkages with them.

The business partner's leadership knowledge can be initially developed through their positive engagement within their role. Lessons learned or skills acquisition may then be taken forward into their next role. The increasing competences acquired may also provide a foundation for the aspiration to becoming an effective leader at some point in the future.

Professional development

The business partner's professional development can be tracked through a variety of organizational planning tools and processes. What is more complex and difficult to measure is the personal self-development that might not be disclosed within a formal organizational planning process. This self-awareness and deeper personal understanding as result of these experiences, now follows.

Personal development

Personal development is the activity of establishing an action plan based on knowledge, standards, behaviours and objectives within the context of a role within an organization. The PDP (personal development plan) may include a statement of the business partner's ambitions, competences, knowledge and skills, and how these can be further enhanced. This will then support a pathway for their career to be developed further.

Within a business partner/stakeholder relationship there may be implied personal development opportunities. This is in effect the psychological contract between the two parties in relation to their joint emotional support for each other. This will include compassion, empathy, fairness, respect, and trust for each other. When the softer skills are in place, the mutual aims and goals can be potentially accelerated, as there is less conflict resolution to take place within the relationship and more time focused on achieving the targets required.

The softer skills and expectations with stakeholders

The softer skills that are required for the business partner are effectively embodied in the social skills within a psychological contract. A psychological contract can be defined as the perceptions of two parties, of what their mutual requirements and expectations are towards each other. These requirements will often be informal and imprecise. These will be influenced from:

- past occurrences
- current experiences
- expectations for the future.

There are three levels that may impact upon the personal obligations, expectations and personal development between a business partner and the stakeholders they support.

- First, at a macro level the culture of where the relationships are based will have an impact upon the relationship e.g. different country values vary and should be understood and respected.
- Second, personal contracts will be partly influenced at an organizational level through corporate values, often defined and articulated within the organization's mission and vision statements.
- Third, and perhaps the most significant, is the individual social interactions at a micro or individual level that will influence the behavioural norms and will have a strong impact upon personal development. A positive personal contract will provide for self-insights and then personal development of the business partner. The negative aspect of these will impair personal development.

These individual interpretations of personal expectations may have a weak correlation and will have little resemblance to what the perceived organizational formal obligations are. However, they do lead to a deeper understanding between parties for personal development opportunities. Imprecise and ill-defined personal relationships are a fundamental part of the continuous relationships between business partners and stakeholders. Positive personal, cultural, trust, and professional ethics are important in developing personal and productive relationships and the development of increasing levels of trust.

Trust

The development of trust

Building trust with key stakeholders is a vital outcome of business partner relationships. Trust has elements of both logical and emotional perspectives.

> Simonin (1997) classifies the benefits of collaborative business relationships into two categories: tangible and intangible. He cites generating additional profits, improving market share, and sustaining competitive advantage as examples of tangible benefits and learning specific skills and developing competencies as intangible benefits. Traditionally, the tangible benefits of collaboration have received the greatest attention from researchers; however recently an increasing number of researchers have turned their attention to the intangible benefits of collaborative business relationships.
> (Palakshappa & Gordon, 2007)

A logical perspective occurs when there is an assessment of the quantitative probabilities or potential advantages for each party of the business relationship. This is based on hard deliverables that include improved business performance, the provision of analysis, business reports or information; there is a degree of certainty and predictability, which raises the expectation that the business partner and stakeholder will deliver outputs or outcomes in a predictable manner.

The above defines 'what' trust delivers, the key challenge is 'how' can trust be developed within the early stages of the emerging relationship between a business partner and their relevant stakeholders. Figure 7.7 shows the key features that will support the establishment and the continuing development of a culture of trust between both parties. The four key elements for trust: value, predictability, reciprocity, and vulnerability are illustrated in the circle of trust.

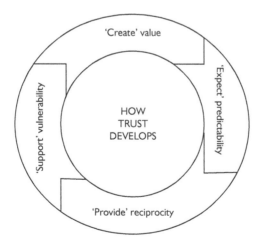

Figure 7.7 How trust develops

Value

From a tangible perspective, value exchange is a basic paradigm for any organization. For example, a product is bought for money; both parties are then satisfied with the value exchange. However, business partner relationships are predominantly based on intangible factors, this then becomes a more complex level of value exchange. On an intangible basis, both parties are unlikely to have the awareness of what is being received or expected. In addition, neither party will have full knowledge between themselves of how they will work or operate with each other. This can cause a deviation between expectations, however fact and evidence based advice will support the closing of this initial gap. Substantive facts rather than opinions will facilitate the initial development of trust. The business partner value exchange can then be further developed upon its level of predictability. Creating value through joint outputs and outcomes is the fundamental key for business partnering relationship to grow and develop.

Predictability

A normal part of any business relationship is to be routinely forecasting into the future. Both internal and external models of the business environment, experiences and business analysis, are utilized to predict what occur in the future. This allows evaluation and preparation to deal with business threats or opportunities. Predictability supports trust in that there is a degree of expectation both logically and emotionally of what is likely to occur in a wide range of circumstances.

Reciprocity

The delay that may occur within reciprocal arrangements can create a high level of uncertainty, which can then be mitigated through levels of predictability. What makes companies and business partnering relationships function is the continuing value exchange and degree of predictability. However, intangible value exchange is not just about an immediate transfer of support, this can be delayed, however the outcome will be paid back some time in the future. The expectation is that both parties will reciprocate support with each other at some point in the future. This becomes particularly important, otherwise the relationship is a one-way process of support. A simple formula for creating trust is to provide a continuing equality of two-way reciprocation. It establishes the dynamic for providing the expectation of receiving an unspecified benefit in the indeterminate near future e.g. favourable feedback, bonuses, team engagement, and job enrichment.

Vulnerability

From an emotional perspective the vulnerabilities of the individual stakeholder or business partner may be exposed within the belief systems that neither party will not take any unreasonable advantage or personal benefit from each other. This is based upon qualitative features such as being at ease with each other and having mutual respect, again there is a degree of certainty and predictability which concludes that an individual will act and behave in a predictable manner. When trust is provided, there is an expectation that a tangible or intangible provision will create an expectation of reciprocation at some point in the future. This can create a degree of vulnerability, as a future expectation may not be met. Another example may be that the business partner working standards may be slipping due to personal circumstances e.g. family bereavement, illness, and personal problems. Supporting exposed vulnerabilities with confidence and respect will support a deepening of trust between parties.

In summary, trust within business partnering will be an outcome when value is created, within expected predictability, reciprocity being provided, and any vulnerability is fully supported. Personal and stakeholder team assessments will work effectively if this is conducted by a two-way discussion in an open and transparent manner based on mutual trust. The outcome of trust will have logical, emotional and ethical features within the business relationship.

Ethics

The importance of personal and professional ethics

The personal and professional outcomes of ethics will support aspiring business partners in attaining leadership roles.

The term ethics is applied to any system or theory of moral values or principles that involves systemizing, defending and recommending concepts of right and wrong behaviour. Several professional bodies will have a code of ethics that will determine the scope of the standards that should be expected by a business partner, and where relevant these should be strictly adhered to. However, all business partners may not be members or affiliated to any professional body or association. In this situation there are several models that can be utilized for the business partner to consider and apply.

Fundamental principles

A code of ethics may be made up of five fundamental principles:

1 *Integrity:* being straightforward, honest and truthful in all professional and business relationships, and not being associated with any information that one believes contains a materially false or misleading statement, or which is misleading by omission.
2 *Objectivity:* not allowing bias, conflict of interest or the influence of other people to override a professional judgment.
3 *Professional competence and due care:* an on-going commitment to a level of professional knowledge and skill. This is based on current developments

in practice, legislation, and techniques. Team members must also have appropriate training and supervision.

4   *Confidentiality:* not disclosing professional information without specific permission or a legal or professional duty to do so.

5   *Professional behaviour:* complying with relevant laws and regulations and also avoiding any action that could negatively affect the profession.

(CGMA, 2015)

Threats and risks

There are potential threats or risks to these fundamental principles. A broad range of relationships and circumstances may create threats. When a relationship or circumstance creates a threat, such a threat could compromise, or could be perceived to compromise compliance with the fundamental principles above. A circumstance or relationship may create more than one threat, and a threat may affect compliance with more than one fundamental principle.

Threats fall into one or more of the following categories:

1   *Self-interest threat:* this is the threat that a financial or other interest will inappropriately influence judgment or behaviour.

2   *Self-review threat:* this is the threat that a business partner will not appropriately evaluate the results of a previous judgment made or activity or service performed by another individual within the business partners firm or employing organization.

3   *Advocacy threat:* this includes the threat that the business partner will promote a stakeholder's position to the point that the business partner's objectivity is compromised.

4   *Familiarity threat:* this threat takes into account a long or close relationship with a client or employer.

5   *Intimidation threat:* this threat is when an individual is deterred from acting objectively because of actual or perceived pressures, including attempts to exercise undue influence over the business.

(CGMA, 2015)

There are increasing pressures upon organizations upon ethical attitudes and behaviours. This outcome is a key attribute for all roles and corporate governance.

Case study: Ethics

This case study relates to how the ethics of the business partner might be under pressure from a stakeholder. The scope of the case study includes many of the points reviewed in the previous section.

The context of the case study

- The business partner (BP) was newly promoted from outside the organization into a new start-up company within a larger group.
- The group director (GD) made the appointment.
- The business partner had a young family and a large mortgage.
- There was a six-month probationary period in place at the discretion of the managing director (MD).
- The MD was autocratic and uncompromising in his style of management.
- The MD and GD had a strong business relationship.

What occurred within the first three months

- The GD on ad hoc basis had prepared the monthly information for two months; the BP reviewed the information on arrival and identified it was inaccurate, incomplete and it overstated favourably the position of the start-up.
- The next month was the year-end results, albeit for three months, and the BP was responsible for completing these.
- In private, the MD strongly verbally stated to the BP that he must meet his year-end targets and for any 'problems' to be rolled over into the next trading year. The motivation for this was his annual bonus.
- The BP acted ethically and presented the correct trading results initially to the GD, who appointed the BP, for a second opinion. The facts and information were provided in detail and full evidence of the results for the year. The BP did highlight that some of the discrepancies in the first two months related to the GD, who acknowledged he had insufficient time to deal with them at the time. The GD did acknowledge the degree of detail, analysis and professionalism of the information pack relating to the trading results.
- The BP requested that the GD contact the MD and confirm that the results for the three months were accurate and that he fully supported them, he had appointed the BP and wished for the GD to express his support for the BP in his probationary period, to the MD. This took place.
- The bonus was not paid in full to the MD. The auditors accepted the results and probationary period was completed successfully.

The key points

- The BP used the situational analysis impact priority matrix to determine the priorities that needed to be attended to.
- There was a significant implied threat of self-interest if the MD's bonus was not paid and that the probationary period would not end favourably for the BP.

- The BP exploited the familiarity threat between the GD and MD favourably.
- In summary ethics may be easy to read and consider. The defining moment is: 'are you prepared to put your position and employment on the line for your professional ethics' (the author was the BP in this case study).

Setting up a business partnering program

One of the potential outcomes of the general business-partnering model may include the establishment of a new business-partnering programme. In addition, existing programmes may benefit from improvements or changes that could be implemented as new knowledge, skills, and competences that may provide new insights from the general business-partnering model.

The advent of the business partner is not new. However, there is a current growing trend in its application nationally and also globally across multinational organizations and the various models that might apply.

Models for establishing business-partnering programs

We now review what are the drivers for establishing business partners programmes. An overview of this can be initially considered in Figure 7.8.

Fundamental drivers for the establishment of a business partner program will include executive leadership, organizational requirements, and acceptance; these can be further categorized into moderate and high influencing factors. One of the salient points for the success of any of the models will be senior leadership and stakeholder buy in to the model being implemented.

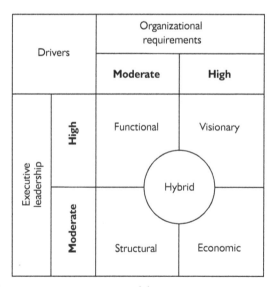

Figure 7.8 Business partner programme models

The structural model

The structural model is when the organizational requirements and the leadership for driving programs are moderate.

Features for this category are:

- It is reacting to events within the organization; an example of this would be the establishment of shared services, which will impact upon the traditional roles within an organization.
- There is a shortage of skills within the organization.
- The organizational demands for the business partner services are moderate and sharing resources across different geographies is more efficient.

The economic model

The economic model occurs when there are high organizational requirements and the executive leadership is moderate.

Features for this category are:

- Outside pressures, e.g. regulatory intervention, necessitate change.
- There is a drive to make the organization a 'flatter structure'.
- There are cost reduction pressures.
- The principle driver is efficiency as opposed to effectiveness.
- The business partner program is established as a reaction to events and pressures.

The functional model

The functional model occurs when there is a moderate organizational demand, however the functional leadership is a significant driver of change.

Features for this category are:

- There is proactive leadership as opposed to reacting to events.
- It will be part of a holistic approach of the whole effectiveness of the function.
- The level of collaboration and engagement with stakeholders will be high.
- There will be a drive to develop talent for future functional leadership roles.
- Both improved efficiency and effectiveness will be sought.
- Business partners from traditional specialism may have difficulty in transiting to their new roles, e.g. finance.

The visionary model

The visionary model occurs when there are significant organizational demands resulting from; strong opinions, values or beliefs from the CEO or functional lead.

Features for this category are:

- A senior executive will set up the establishment of the business-partnering programme, they will seek a strategic long-term view.
- The model will be applied to the whole organization as opposed to a fragmented approach by the differing functional models.
- It will be part of a strategic and sustainable approach to the whole organization.
- There will be a drive to develop talent for future organizational leadership roles by creating a culture of forward looking, evolution, personal development, growth, and new idea creation.
- The business partner talent development will be across several key functions.
- Rotation across functions and geographies will be part of the development, this will support a sustainable culture, create powerful internal networks and become the development pool for senior positions.
- It will improve the efficiency, effectiveness, and enhance the business, or organizational operating model.

Hybrid model

The hybrid model will apply when several features from the structured, economic, functional and organizational models might apply and may be relevant to the establishment of the business-partnering program.

Proactive planned business-partnering programmes

The functional model and visionary models have a greater level of proactive planning. These approaches to establishing a business partner programme will therefore have common stages to them, and these can be defined and explained as:

Leadership insight

This should include:

- a vision by a functional or organizational leader for proactive change;
- there will be an insight to proactively develop talent;
- seeking effectiveness and added value for the organization;
- a strategic perspective;
- developing the organizational messages and why the step change is taking place.

Developing organizational buy in

This should include:

- initial engagement and discussions with senior stakeholders;

- training stakeholders to get the best out of their business partners;
- consultation and collaboration where the business partners may be placed;
- the impact upon the continuing, transferring, or outsourcing of activities;
- cascading the engagement with the organization, which may include:
  - the development of questionnaires
  - workshops
  - one-to-one meetings with key influencers and stakeholders
  - organizational and team briefings.

Effective execution

This will include:

- a formal project being established including:
  - the appointment of a project manager
  - quad of aims being developed
  - formal plans with milestones
  - project monitoring
  - effective close out.
- cross-functional steering groups that the project will report to.

Sustainability

This may include:

- reviewing the lessons learned from the implementation;
- appraising the legacy issues arising from the implementation;
- the development of a talent programme that will support continuation of the business partnering programme;
- planned and professional transition from a project phase to a business-as-usual management;
- clear role clarity of who has primary responsibility for what (e.g. is the stakeholder responsible for the accuracy of forecasts or is it finance?); if the stakeholder has the primary accountability, then should the finance business partner be responsible for explaining the variance of forecasts from actual results – this type of accountability dilemma will apply to all supporting functions.

Concluding perspectives

The general model of business partnering will be impacted by which business-partnering model has been established or predominates. Where a proactive and planned approach is taken by the function or organization, then a new business partner is likely to have received structured support through all six stages. Where a reactive method has been implemented, the expectation is what the business partner will immediately deliver is Stage 4 of the general model. This may necessitate 'a learn as you go' approach. In these circumstances some of the methods in the first three stages, if considered and retrospectively applied, may support learning opportunities, and enhance the effective delivery of the business partner.

Governance

The governance models to be considered and enhanced

One of the general business-partnering outcomes is to review, improve or change the governance arrangements that are in place. Potential amendments may be dependent on the governance model that may be put in place.

Three examples of governance models will include:

- functional (which will be the most common)
- inter-organizational
- intra-organizational.

Functional business partnering

The functional executive or director will approve the governance model and methods for functional business partnering. With the increasing trends on organizations of legislation, technical requirements, complexity, increasing use of technology self-service, and resource constraints, there is an accelerating trend in the use of business partnering. The organizational model had its origins from the human resources function.

Several functional business-partnering models have been previously outlined and these included:

- finance
- human resources (HR)
- information technology (IT)
- procurement.

The key differential features to be considered between functions in relation to business partnering are:

- different functions have different perspectives;
- the legitimized use and interpretation is different;
- the usage and application varies;
- there is a degree of variability with their relevant professional requirements;
- business requirements will influence the rate of evolution and adoption of business partnering;
- the culture of the organization will impact business partnering.

Intra organizational business partnering

This will likely evolve from the functional model. The governance model is probably controlled and exercised below executive or board level; however the framework will have been agreed at that executive level. There are increasing trends for organizations to reduce cost, improve technologies, and introduce flexible working and agile working changes. Therefore intra organizational business partnering to meet business long-term and short-term requirements is increasing. The organizational model had its originations based on using a decreasing pool of talent and resources to meet long-term increasing organizational needs.

Inter-organizational business partnering

The governance model will be controlled and exercised at executive or board level. In addition to any internal requirements, there will be a demand to support the supply chain, or customers for effective business-to-business engagement. The relevant executive will direct where these resources are best placed. The business-to-business model had its origin in a legal, contractual and due diligence organizational framework.

Partnerships are two or more individuals or entities commencing a cooperative relationship based on:

1 mutual aim or prospects that support specific aims that are difficult to achieve individually;
2 where individuals or entities do not have the financial or resources to deliver their different objectives.

Accountability incorporates the issues or influences that affect significant choices or decisions. Decision-making power also determines the actions that can be undertaken. Governance affects the structures, processes, and rules and traditions of the organization.

Accountability can consist of these distinct features:

• compliance: this is being held to account to rules and regulations;
• transparency: this is providing open accountability;
• responsiveness: this is taking accountability in a timely manner;

Governance and accountability are significant drivers of partnership performance, particularly those that are larger, formalized, and resource intensive. Simply put, accountability drives decisions, which in turn drives performance and outcomes, implying that partnerships governed by clear accountability structures, processes and norms aligned to its mission will have enhanced performance and outcomes. Partnerships have particular governance and accountability issues and needs, only some of which can be addressed by lessons drawn from business, public sector, and civil society organizations.

(Palakshappa, and Gordon, 2007)

There is a maxim that contracts between organizations should only be looked at when things go wrong. Often, business-to-business relationships are not proactively designed, they often evolve reactively and this can lead to poor control, unclear responsibilities and unclear expectations. This can create issues later due to legal, contractual, and due diligence requirements that may evolve later. The focus is on what needs to occur rather than how the inter-organizational relationships operate on an on-going daily basis. The focus tends to be on what are the requirements rather than how they will be governed.

Additional features

Despite the differences of the above models, there can be common features of application and these will be influenced from corporate goals and culture. Three additional features will include:

1   outcome-based partnerships, which are strategic and focused on the long term;
2   regulation-based partnerships, which are flexible and tactical by nature;
3   resourcing partnerships, which are short term and operational by nature.

Outcome-designed partnerships are usually designed by top-down guidelines geared to use internal resources in the delivery of products and services. Their aim is to be outcome-based, with the whole enterprise robustly concentrated on the requirements of the key stakeholders. The support of internal partners are focused upon the overall corporate outcomes. For example, an accountant being placed within a marketing team to enhance brand value.

Regulation-partnerships are normally coalitions of stakeholders and subject-matter experts to define, develop, implement, measure and monitor the formal requirements for working together. The primary orientation of these partnerships will be on the individuals within the organization who comply with the regulations or rules that have been established. This will include the monitoring of financial, legal and reputational risks and concerns. The business-partnering relationships have to be diligent as processes change and improve, for example, an end-to-end business process across functions will require consistent and compatible rules.

Resourcing partnerships are generally made possible through agreement rather than enforcement; these might be where there are resource shortfalls within the organization to meet business targets. Their primary orientation is project or temporary based, with a strong emphasis of supporting the stakeholder with a shortfall of resources. The expectations of the stakeholders may be feebly related within business partnership relationships, for example, transferring human resources from daily maintenance activities to work within a capital investment project.

There will be blended variations of the above models and features that are in use within organizations and these will be additionally dependent on the following variables:

- time: is this a short-, medium- or long-term requirement or need;
- resource restrictions;
- cost constraints;
- organizational goals;
- priorities.

Conceptually the alignment of functional business, the inter-organization, and the intra organization and partnering models should provide enhanced organizational outcomes. However, in practice, if they are misaligned or fragmented in their approach and style there may need to be a re-examination of what governance arrangements should be considered. Poor or ineffective governance arrangements may constrain the engagement within the organization.

Lessons learned

Lessons learned is an outcome that has been used to end or close projects and it can also usefully be deployed at the end of the placement of a business partner assignment. In addition, this process could be deployed to evaluate business-partnering programmes in total on a periodic basis, for example, annually. Organizations may deploy exit interviews for those leaving the organization. If in place, the same process can be used for internal promotions. The primary intent of the lessons learned approach is to positively improve the next cycle of the business partnering process.

Prepare

Preparation is important to enhance the positive outcomes of the close of a business-partnering placement. There are several features that will support this and these will include:

- Initial preparation should commence with information gathering.
- The categorization of lessons learned should be agreed upon.
- The lessons learned document should be designed, developed, and circulated in advance.
- Deciding the form of the meeting to take place. Options could include using existing processes e.g. one-to-one, team meetings, exit interviews, or a one-off meeting.
- Individual preparation for the meeting. If no thought is given in advance to lessons learned, it is likely that many details may be omitted.

- Planning and scheduling the attendance of the meeting. In addition to the exiting business partner, this could include the stakeholder and functional manager and HR.
- An agenda should be established that sets clear boundaries.

Acceptance

The acceptance of the issues identified should be shared in a timely and dependable manner. The categorization of the issues should include the impact of, failures, successes and recommendations that should be applied. The process is to concentrate upon what can be improved and is actionable, and should avoid blame, negativity, any perspective of loss of control, or lack of ownership.

Engagement at the meeting

The findings of the issues should also be verified and communicated before any meeting takes place. The findings should consider the following:

- consistency with other lessons learnt documents;
- whether any organisational standards are met;
- the pertinent level of detail;
- the relevant classification of issues;
- the knowledge area that the lesson applies to must be agreed.

An example of this is shown in Figure 7.9.

Category	Issue	Problem or success	Impact	Recommendation
Personal	Poor screen of individuals	Concerns with stakeholders	Poor expectations by business partner	Improve preparation
Team	Briefing of stakeholder team	Poor assimilation	Confusion of how the role impact the rest of the team	Acceptance needs enhancing
Stakeholder	Stakeholder overloaded	Lack of briefing to business partner	Informal expectations	Engagement process need documenting
Organizational	Delivery outcomes not clear	Over-delivery on expectations which cost too much	Specification very good, cost escalation	Delivery measurements to be put in place
Programme	Lack of support to business partners	Business partners going 'native'	Functions concerned with standards slipping	Change criteria to be developed to enhance matrix responsibilities

Figure 7.9 Examples of lessons learned

Delivery

The completion of the lessons learned document and its subsequent circulation is the required output of the meeting.

Change

The recommendations from the document will require changes to be undertaken.

The lessons learned from the business partner placement can be used as references for future placements and should have sufficient information to support the preparation stage for the next incoming business partner.

Outcomes

It is imperative that the document for lessons learned is completed at the close of the business partner placement. This will support the personal development of the business partner in their new role and improved team engagement with the stakeholder and their teams. Where required, it will support the induction of incoming new business partner. The lessons learned approach does take a small investment of time. If it does not take place there is a risk of intellectual property being lost as the business partner exits and therefore mistakes being repeated.

Chapter summary

The outcomes for any operating model will impact the personal outcomes for the business partner and these will include their own financial and non-financial rewards. Additionally the business partner's personal development, trust and their ethical standards will have been enhanced. The alignment of these to the stakeholder and their teams towards organizational alignment create a powerful line of sight for the outcomes being aimed for or targeted. The review of how knowledge, skills, and competences relate to current and new operating models is considered. These also support the entity outcomes relating to organizational, stakeholder and team expectations. The personal outcomes for the business partner are interrelated with the stakeholder, their teams and organizational successful outcomes.

In addition to completing this chapter the six stages of the general model has now been completed. In summary the general model of business partnering has six stages and these are:

1 prepare (Chapter 2)
2 engage (Chapter 3)
3 accept (Chapter 4)
4 deliver (Chapter 5)
5 change (Chapter 6)
6 outcome (Chapter 7).

References

CGMA (2012) 'Relevance regained: Performance management in shared service centres' Retrieved 8 March 2015 from www.cgma.org/Resources/Reports/Pages/Relevance-regained-performance-management.aspx

CGMA (2015) 'CGMA code of ethics' Retrieved 30 November 2015 from http://www.cgma.org/AboutCGMA/Pages/code-of-ethics.aspx

Duignan, P. (2009) 'Using outcomes theory to solve important conceptual and practical problems in evaluation, monitoring and performance management systems', American Evaluation Association Conference, Orlando, Florida, 11–14 November

Fourman, L.S. and Jones, J. (1997) 'Job enrichment in extension', *Journal of Extension*, 35(5), retrieved 8 March 2015 from http://joe.org/joe/1997October/iw1.html

Hackman, J.R. (1987). 'The design of work teams'. *Handbook of Organizational Behavior*. Cambridge, MA:Harvard Business School Press.

Hackman, J.R. (2002). *Leading Teams: Setting the Stage For Great Performances.* Boston, MA: Harvard Business School Press.

Kotter, John P. (1996) *Leading Change*. Cambridge, MA: Harvard Business School Press.

Palakshappa, N. and Gordon, M.E. (2007) 'Collaborative business relationships', *Journal of Small Business and Enterprise Development*, 14(2) 264–279.

Schneider, B. and Bowen, D.E. (1985). 'Employee and customer perceptions of service in banks: replication and extension', *Journal of Applied Psychology*, 70(3): 423–433.

Simonin, B.L. (1997) 'The importance of collaborative knows-how: an empirical test of the learning organization', *Academy of Management Journal* 40(5): 1150–1174.

8 The final recap

A recap: a summary of what has been said.

An investment in knowledge pays the best interest.

Benjamin Franklin

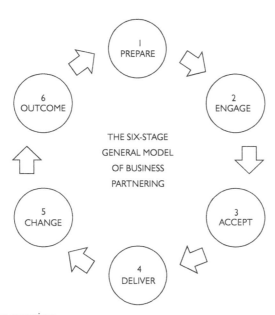

Figure 8.1 Recap overview

The final recap

The final recap will include a review of the previous seven chapters. In addition, there are propositions that are being presented for further exploration, analysis, and future research.

Summary points by chapter and propositions

Introduction (Chapter 1)

The general business model applies to the six life-cycle stages to business partnering. There are different approaches and styles for business partnering. The styles include control, service and advisory. It reviews the different business functions' perspective of business partnering. The chapter explains the importance of business partnering for the individual, function and organizational level.

The propositions for research, review, and consideration in this chapter include:

1 Organizations in which stakeholders and business partners engage in explicit dialogue about the different styles at which employees enter into the business partnering process and how they will encounter fewer perceived problems and constraints than those organizations that do not engage in such dialogue.
2 Business partnering has been legitimized by a variety of professional bodies and yet no general model of business partnering outside their professional scope has yet been developed that can be unconditionally applied or accepted to other professions.
3 The general model of business partnering and its six stages can be universally used to a varied extent in both internal and external organizational requirements that will enhance enterprise value.

Prepare (Chapter 2)

To prepare is to make (something) ready for use. There are several governance models that can be considered and this will influence the initial induction process of business partners. A strategic review will dictate what priorities are required; this will be supported by relevant knowledge, skills, and competences of the business partner. An assessment of personal values, beliefs, ethics, culture, personal, team assessments, and trust will enhance outputs to stakeholders. Models and different styles of business partnering will influence stakeholder's positive engagement and the initial impact of the business partner. The requirement for the personal responsibility for self-learning and induction is also outlined. The power of the stakeholder and how this impacts the stakeholder and teams will influence the style that should be adopted by the business partner. Reviewing the organizational culture and situation will determine the impacts and priorities that the business partner should prepare and then focus upon.

The propositions for research, review, and consideration for this chapter include:

1 The assimilation of the optimum governance model for business partnering and how this will impact the induction process, and then the

business partner's behaviours and attitudes to their stakeholder and their organizational expectations.
2   The integration of personal values, beliefs, ethics and culture for the business partner are more likely to result in a deepening application of skills and competences that will build trust with stakeholders into engaging in a positive psychological contract with them.
3   The power base of the business partner and stakeholder are naturally differentiated, however, when aligned, they can realize significant incremental benefits to the organization.

Engage (Chapter 3)

To engage is to occupy or attract someone's attention. The requirement for effective engagement includes the setting of expectations and dealing with any initial conflicts. The models and their features that are utilized for in-depth engagement will influence where the business partner may also be optimally placed. The consideration and complexities of working within matrix relationships will influence how the business partner's aims are developed to create enterprise value and enable them to excel in their role. There is a requirement to understand the complexity of engagement on a multi-dimensional level and the different models that might be adopted will influence the style of engagement. Effective engagement should also consider the impact of softer issues that will build and support effective relationships. Working in a matrix relationship for the business partner in some form is probable. Therefore, understanding the legitimacy, urgency, power, and how this impacts the relationship then may become a critical component of effective engagement.

The propositions for research, review, and consideration for this chapter include:

1   The development and deepening of softer and qualitative aspects of the business partner relationship with stakeholders is likely to result in positive quantitative outcomes.
2   The business partner requires to set initial expectations to all stakeholders, even though this is likely to result in short term conflict within a matrix relationship; this will support long-term mutual support based on trust and openness.
3   The business partner's absorption of the stakeholder's legitimacy, urgency and power will be positively correlated to how they will react to them.

Acceptance (Chapter 4)

Acceptance is to consent, receive or undertake something offered. Before final integrated acceptance can be attained, interpersonal and organization conflict invariably will occur. Although conflicts occur, there are positive traits and models that will facilitate earlier resolution; both participants are part of the initial problem and then the final solution. The appraisal of conflict includes a review of what causes them. The process and methods of acceptance will support the integration of team norms to all members. When fully integrated, acceptance is attained, the delivery of outputs and outcomes will be enhanced and this supports positive resolution of both personal and organizational conflicts. Acceptance of the business partner will be enhanced by appreciation of the differing thinking styles and models that can be applied. Full integration of the business partner into teams that deliver excellent results is a primary feature of full and complete acceptance.

The propositions for research, review, and consideration for this chapter include:

1   Acceptance by the business partner is likely to require an initial degree of conflict; the speed of resolution of these in the short term will predict the salience of conflict in the long term.
2   There will be a positive correlation with being accepted when personal and team norms are aligned to a common purpose rather than them being fragmented.
3   An understanding of different thinking styles will predict the behaviours that the business partner can anticipate and this will support the adoption of strategies to accommodate and accept them.

Delivery (Chapter 5)

Delivery is to provide something that is promised or expected. The business delivery and operating models that are in use will all make an impact. The constraints and enablers that are in place will influence the scope of delivery. Delivery is a key expectation the stakeholder will have upon the business partner to support. This includes the review of business, delivery and operating models that can be applied. It defines the type of delivery that includes goals, aims, targets, outcomes, outputs and objectives with both the constraints and enablers that might apply. Within these delivery types a variety of potential delivery models are then considered. These vary from strategic goals to individual and team objectives. The fundamental paradigm for the business partner is their value proposition and contribution towards effective delivery.

Delivery is to sustain the 'as-is' position and does not seek to change it. The prime aim of change is to progress to a new state. Improvement can either be part of the current 'as-is' focus or the new 'to-be' model. The relevance is that the models described in Chapters 5 and 6, depending on the maturity and circumstance can be applied to delivery, improvement, or change. The knowledge and skill of applying them to the optimum circumstance will vary between organizations and this is where the competence and expertise of the business partner becomes critical for what, when, why, and where the methods are best applied. The decision to determine which model should apply will be determined by these factors.

The propositions for research, review, and consideration for this chapter include:

1 The immediate requirements for stakeholder delivery will be positively related to the current 'as-is' position objectives and outputs.
2 The obligations of the stakeholder upon the business partner for improved outcomes will most likely be assigned to the current 'as-is' situation or improving the current state, rather than being assigned to changing them to a new model or method of operating.
3 The circumstances, maturity and business environment will determine which models or methods are optimally applied to deliver, improve or change the outcomes required.

Change (Chapter 6)

Change is to progress from an old 'as-is' state towards a new 'to-be' state. It provides a line of sight to examples of change approaches that can be applied. What causes and drives change, what resistance might be expected, and how to overcome them are reviewed. More positively, the enablers of positive and successful change have been defined and explored with relevant methodologies that can be applied. Change is powered by strategic, tactical and operational causes; these impact the attainment of goals, aims, targets, outcomes, outputs and objectives. Applying the optimum change model(s) will enhance success and then mitigate the risks of failure.

The propositions for research, review, and consideration for this chapter include:

1 Knowledge and skill applied by both the stakeholder and business partner to change from an 'as-is' position to an enhanced new 'to-be' model is likely to occur when effective change models and methods are applied.
2 When the internal changes are slower than external expectations, enterprise value may be opportunities lost; the opposite will also apply.
3 The use of change methodologies is more likely to speed and embed change quicker than not utilizing them.

Outcome (Chapter 7)

The outcomes of any operating model will impact the personal outcomes for the business partner and these will include their own financial and non-financial rewards. Additionally the business partner's personal development, trust, and their ethical standards are enhanced. The alignment of these to the stakeholder and their teams towards organizational alignment create a powerful line of sight for the outcomes being aimed for or targeted. How the knowledge, skills and competences relate to current and new operating models are reviewed. These support the entity outcomes relating to organizational, stakeholder, and team expectations. The personal outcomes for the business partner are interrelated with the stakeholder, their teams and organizational successful outcomes.

The propositions for research, review, and consideration for this chapter include:

1   The personal outcomes for the business partner will be aligned to the results of the stakeholder, their teams and the organization, rather than having no correlation with them.
2   The entity outcomes are likely to be enhanced with positive long-term financial and operational successes when trust and ethics are embedded as part of the culture.
3   A common line of sight upon the required outcomes by the business partner, stakeholder and their teams will predict faster attainment of the required outcomes rather than a fragmented or diffused approach.

How to be an efficient and effective business partner

As outlined in the earlier chapters of this book, there are several attributes, features and elements that relate to efficient and effective business partnering. In my opinion there are two simple parts that interlink to achieve effective business partnering. First, these are what the business partner performs in relation to their expert knowledge, skills, and competences for their stakeholders. Second and equally important is how they apply these through their emotional intelligence, acceptance, and positive engagement with their stakeholders. The combined impact of 'what and how' will enhance the delivery of aims, targets, goals, objectives, outcomes, or outputs that are being sought (Figure 8.2).

A more detailed review of what and how an effective business partner should use their knowledge and skills now follows.

Figure 8.2 Ying and yang of what and how

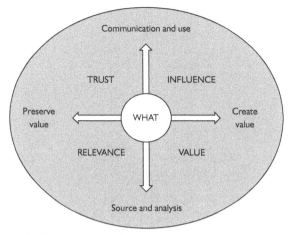

Figure 8.3 What is business partnering?

What is efficient business partnering?

We now examine the key attributes, features, and elements of what an efficient business partner should be cognizant of.

The model in Figure 8.3 highlights:

- Communication is a key attribute that a business partner uses to deliver and influence. The use of the information, analysis, or data by the stakeholder is of equal importance. The stakeholder will need a level of acceptance and trust with the business partner for the communication to be acted upon.
- Creation of value by the business partner involves supporting stakeholders and their teams that they operate within, towards added value delivery or enhanced outcomes. The team effectiveness will be influenced significantly by the business partner's integration and acceptance.
- The source of the analysis will be based on the business partners expert knowledge and understanding of the enterprise that they operate within.
- The combination and use of both of these elements will support enhanced enterprise value and stakeholder relevance.
- Preserved value is where the operating model is either mature or high performing, or both. To maintain relevant consistency and high performance requires significant trust and mutual team support. Preserving value through excellent, customer service, minimal cost and effective outcomes is the optimum state of what should be delivered.

How is effective business partnering delivered?

We now examine the key attributes, features, and elements of how an effective business partner should apply their competences.

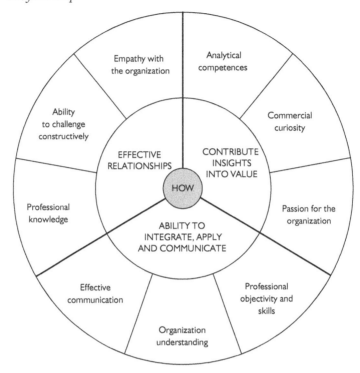

Figure 8.4 How is effective business partnering delivered?

Figure 8.4 highlights three key attributes, these are:

The ability to integrate, apply and communicate

The ability of integration, application, and communication requires professional objectivity and skills to be applied. The expert skills, knowledge, and competences are requirements that the stakeholder will seek. Understanding the organization through its business model and how it operates will help focus where the business partner should integrate their working relationships with individuals and teams.

The combination of the above will help target effective communication.

To develop effective relationships

Effective communication is a feature of effective relationships.

The level of professional knowledge will help support the ability to challenge constructively. A positive approach, rather than a critical one will influence stakeholders and their teams more.

The insights of relationships will then create enhanced empathy with the organization.

To contribute insights that create enterprise value

Analytical competences of an effective business partner combined with commercial curiosity will support enhanced insights into what might be delivered or improved within their existing operating model. The insights may be so powerful that there is acceptance that the operating model should be fundamentally changed. This would indicate a passion for the organization to deliver to new higher standards for customer service, improve cycle times, cash improvements, and compliance expectations or requirements.

A summary of what and how good business partnering is

The models above are a recap and review of what and how efficient and effective business partnering can deliver. The 'what and how' will be impacted by:

- external business environmental influences;
- the pressures of improving or changing the internal operating model;
- the expertise, personality, and style of the business partner;
- the expectations, behaviours, and delivery requirements of the stakeholder and their teams.

These attributes are examples why the business partner relationships are unique to the stakeholder, teams and enterprises that they operate within. The adoption and application of the general model of business partnering and its six stages will enhance outcomes regardless of any uniqueness that the business partner may face.

Final comment

Every book has an ending, this is the certainty of knowledge. The beginning only takes place when you apply the skills that you have learnt. This is the uncertainty of the application of your own true competences and then potential future success.

Glossary

Aim   A purpose or intention for a desired or planned outcome.

As-is   The current state of operating with no changes.

Benchmarking   Evaluating and comparing a service, process or output with an internal or external standard.

Buddy   Someone who will spend time with a new employee, so that they will integrate into the team and organization more quickly.

Business partner   A business partner is an individual who can add value within a team by their specialisms, skills, knowledge, competences and experiences to deliver greater organizational outcomes.

Competence   The use of knowledge and skills in a variety of different and complex situations.

Compliance   Keeping to the internal or external rules and requirements.

Constraints   A limitation or restriction of resources upon delivery.

Customer service   Delivering to the customers needs, this applies to external and internal needs.

Cycle time   The length and time it takes to start and complete a defined activity.

Effectiveness   To add value and do the right thing.

Efficiency   To reduce cost and do it the right way.

Enablers   Provide resources which support or encourage delivery.

Engagement   A positive commitment between employees.

Enhancement   Improvement or augmentation.

Entity   An organization which might be private, public or charitable.

Ethics   The behaviours, conduct and rules that should apply to all the individuals within the entire organization.

Function   A department that supports the core operations, in this book this will specifically apply to finance, human resources, information technology and procurement.

Functional leads   The head of the department who decides upon short-term resource allocation to meet strategic requirements.

Functional perspective   The specialism that the business partner has gained through professional training of acquiring knowledge, skills and competences that they can apply to stakeholders and the organization.

Gantt chart   A visual method of planning used to control.

Goal   A point when delivery of a long-term requirement has been achieved.

Governance   The way the rules, norms and actions are produced, sustained, regulated and employees, teams and function are made accountable to.

Hard skills   Non-people tools and methods that are applied.

Induction programme   A programme to welcome and prepare new employees with knowledge about what is required or expected of them.

Insights   Solutions that present themselves quickly without full detailed analysis.

Knowledge   Familiarity of understanding based on facts, information and is acquired through education or experience.

Legitimacy   The ability to defend with logic, justification or a valid viewpoint.

Mentor   Someone who offers his or her knowledge, wisdom, and advice to someone with less experience.

Methods   Detailed actions or steps that are contained within a particular model (the how and the why).

Mission   The purpose of an organization which defines what, who and how outcomes are delivered.

Models   A theory which has empirical or educational roots and which can be applied (the what).

Objective   A short-term delivery requirement by an individual or team.

Operational   The establishment of short-term actions and resources that will meet tactical and strategic aims.

Outcomes   The medium term results and aggregation of outputs.

Outputs   The sort term results from actions of both inputs and processes.

Paradigm   A typical example or model that is being applied.

Paradoxes   A typical example or model that combines contradictory features or qualities and which may be unacceptable or are self contradictory in nature.

Power   The capability or capacity to instruct or impact the conduct or the performance of others.

Process   A sequence of activities taken to deliver an outcome.

Score cards   Measures the performance of an organization with a mix of financial and non-financial measures.

Skill   Doing something well based on the knowledge which has already been assimilated.

Soft skills   People tools and methods that are applied.

Stakeholder   An individual or group either within or outside an organization that has an interest in the services, outputs or outcomes being provided to them and they also have influence or power over them.

Strategic   The setting of long term aims and determining what are the required actions to achieve them.

Tactical   Mobilizing resources to execute the strategic aims required by defining the medium term the achievements and high level steps that are required.

Targets   A delivery requirement in the short term.

Technique   A skilful or efficient way of doing or achieving something (the what).

To-be   The future state of operating which requires changes from where we are today.

Tool   The specific application or method of a technique (the how and way).

Values   Value underpin the way that employees should interact with each other and how these link to the values and mission of the organization.

Vision   Vision defines an optimal desired future state and provides guidance and inspiration and is focused on five or more years.

World class   Services and processes that are ranked by customers or experts to be amongst the best of the best on a global basis.

Index

When the text is within a table, the number span is in italic, e.g. ARCI (responsible, accountable, consulted, informed) matrix 70–2, *71*
When the text is within a figure, the number span is in bold, e.g. business intelligence (BI) **156**, 157–8

Taylor & Francis eBooks

Helping you to choose the right eBooks for your Library

Add Routledge titles to your library's digital collection today. Taylor and Francis ebooks contains over 50,000 titles in the Humanities, Social Sciences, Behavioural Sciences, Built Environment and Law.

Choose from a range of subject packages or create your own!

Benefits for you

» Free MARC records
» COUNTER-compliant usage statistics
» Flexible purchase and pricing options
» All titles DRM-free.

Benefits for your user

» Off-site, anytime access via Athens or referring URL
» Print or copy pages or chapters
» Full content search
» Bookmark, highlight and annotate text
» Access to thousands of pages of quality research at the click of a button.

REQUEST YOUR **FREE** INSTITUTIONAL TRIAL TODAY

Free Trials Available
We offer free trials to qualifying academic, corporate and government customers.

eCollections – Choose from over 30 subject eCollections, including:

Archaeology	Language Learning
Architecture	Law
Asian Studies	Literature
Business & Management	Media & Communication
Classical Studies	Middle East Studies
Construction	Music
Creative & Media Arts	Philosophy
Criminology & Criminal Justice	Planning
Economics	Politics
Education	Psychology & Mental Health
Energy	Religion
Engineering	Security
English Language & Linguistics	Social Work
Environment & Sustainability	Sociology
Geography	Sport
Health Studies	Theatre & Performance
History	Tourism, Hospitality & Events

For more information, pricing enquiries or to order a free trial, please contact your local sales team: **www.tandfebooks.com/page/sales**

Routledge
Taylor & Francis Group

The home of
Routledge books

www.tandfebooks.com